BURT FRANKLIN: RESEARCH & SOURCE WORKS SERIES 803
Selected Essays in History, Economics & Social Science 289

The Rise of Dennis Hathnaught

THE RISE OF DENNIS HATHNAUGHT

Life of the Common People
Across the Ages as Set
Down in the Great
Books of the
World

By JAMES PHILIP MacCARTHY

BURT FRANKLIN
NEW YORK

Published by LENOX HILL Pub. & Dist. Co. (Burt Franklin)
235 East 44th St., New York, N.Y. 10017
Originally Published: 1915
Reprinted: 1971
Printed in the U.S.A.

S.B.N.: 8337-21615
Library of Congress Card Catalog No.: 77-170961
Burt Franklin: Research and Source Works Series 803
Selected Essays in History,Economics & Social Science 289

To My ·Wife,
JESSIE HOWELL MacCARTHY
Who Assisted Me in Gathering
Material
and Who Typed the Manuscript,
This Book Is Inscribed.

DENNIS HATHNAUGHT'S
GENEALOGICAL TREE

DENNIS HATHNAUGHT RISES TO EXPLAIN.

"The Rise of Dennis Hathnaught" was not written with an eye to obtaining a university degree. It is therefore chatty and informal, rather than painfully scientific and academic. We should not brood too much over the miseries of a dead past when there is so much to be done in the living present. But man may be taught to judge more intelligently of his own time and its problems if he has some idea of past times and their institutions. In this spirit Dennis Hathnaught takes the platform for a short address to his "Fellow Citizens." He will be grateful for any applause he may receive, and hopes that adverse critics will put cotton batting around the bricks they may throw.

Yeoman service for human liberty has been done by persons with a sense of humour. No man who understands the wholesome effect of laughter ever throws a bomb or tries to reform the world by assassination. If the fool that shot J. P. Morgan had brooded less and laughed more, he would not have taken himself so seriously. There has been great injustice in the world, but we have now reached the age of adjustments, when the better elements of Capital and Labour are working earnestly to bring about a more equitable social system.

The Golden Age will not be ushered in by dividing the accumulations of the rich among the poor. It is a question if the vicious, idle, proletariat, who works only under compulsion of economic pressure, is not a greater menace than the unscrupulous capitalist who exploits human labour. It is decreed by the courts eternal that in the sweat of his face man shall earn his bread, and this applies equally as well to John D. Rockefeller as it does to Dennis Hathnaught. The Standard Oil Company would not last a year if Rockefeller dawdled away all his time on the golf links. That is his recreation, just as that of Dennis Hathnaught is bending the elbow with his cronies at Casey's little place on the corner. Every man to his taste.

We cannot reform overnight a world that has been millions of years in the making. There is good basis for the argument that we might lessen the distance to the Millennium if we improved our manners. There is nothing so discouraging as the spectacle of a loud-mouthed economic reformer, whose vocal rearing of the ideal Republic keeps pace with bad manners that find vent in dental archæology—the excavating of a ruined molar with a young sapling—and the editing of fingernails with a pair of pocket scissors.

Let us have patience. Progress is an eternal and an ordered law, and it is written in the stars that we shall not go backward. Every man has his day. The castle and the hut are interchangeable residences. Emerson summarizes the social history of the ages in a stanza:

> The lord is the peasant that was,
> The peasant the lord that shall be;
> The lord is hay, the peasant grass,
> One dry, and one the living tree.

This unceasing struggle operates through the laws of Evolution and Suggestion. A thing that has had no beginning can never have an end. The seeming zenith is but the nadir of new heights. The Ultimate beckons to us but never waits. We are on our way. Whither, only the Fates may tell, and Destiny is not loquacious.

CHAPTER I.

DENNIS HATHNAUGHT'S LOWLY ORIGIN.

Man, that fleck of dust in the Infinite, swelling with pride before the, altar of his Ego and indulging his fancy in self-worship imagines himself a Chantecler, Lord of Creation, Master of Woman and Summoner of the Sun. Engaged as he is in the pursuit of the useless, and eternally struggling for selfish preferment or meaningless pleasure—a spendthrift of time as well as of money—we might imagine the world a great Cosmic Bloomingdale, were it not that here and there one sees the thinker and the doer—the student busy with his experiments, the worker labouring in shop or field.

Eons ago, more years than mind can reckon, this old world of ours was plunging aimlessly through the night of Chaos, and intellectually, it would be plunging through it yet, were it not that in every age, and at intervals almost cyclic there arose men of vision with the teaching and preaching instinct strong within them—in China a Confucius, in Greece a Socrates, in Italy a Savonarola, in Germany a Luther—men with that sublime courage and touch of divinity

that gives them kinship with Christ
and puts the fire of inspiration upon
their words. When such men are abroad
in the land, tyranny and injustice flee
as from a wrath that is overwhelming.

From the time the first man was agitated by the first thought, we have heard
much of Good and of Evil, forces representing some sort of a contest for the
mastery, constantly going on in the
world. Yet there are very few really
good people and very few bad ones. All
men bear the mark of caste, the stigmata
of environment, example and habit, and
the numerosity of the race constitutes a
mediocrity, obsessed by the fetish of
prestige and eternally aping the manners
and pattering the words of other men.
It is a physiological-biological phenomenon that the vast majority of men and
women come into the world with still
born brains—from the cradle to the
grave exhibiting in their lives, the static
monotony of unchanging sameness. One
cannot be said to be truly good, unless
his whole course of action is characterized by sacrifice and disinterested living,
with never a thought of approbation, ap-
preciation or emolument. No one that
shows remorse can be said to be truly
bad.

Rational and normal man may be divided into three classes—the Progressive,
the Lack-alert and the Dumbwit.

The Progressive has the instinct of
personal leadership and acts upon his
own initiative. His only authority is ex-

perience. He is like the Monad of Leibnitz, the universe in miniature.

The Lack-alert does well under instruction, but must always be directed. He reverences authority, even in the face of his own experience and better judgment. Tradition, Father's politics and Mother's religion are all sufficient for this simple child of nature. There isn't the cream of an idea on the top of his bottle; he is a skim-milk thinker. Par excellence he is the Conventionarian.

The Dumbwit acts only under orders and must be driven to his task like the galley slave. Trying to get ideas into his head is like signalling to Mars. He is the backbone of the Caste system— thinks men are born into classes and that they must always remain so. With the Lack-alert, he is the great breeding ground of true snobbery, despising his own kind and deferential to those whom he looks upon as of the better classes. He laughs long and 'oudly when the Man with the New Idea finds his way to King Ignorance barred by the two trusty guardsmen, Prejudice and Bigotry, and is subjected to the badgering of the King's impish children, Little Pooh-Pooh and Taint-so.

Intelligence is as rare as radium and man, all but mummified by acquiescence in traditional authority, grows slowly into fullness of the Spirit and an understanding of the higher life and its significance. What is popularly called intelligence is more often cunning, shrewdness, sagacity. True intelligence is vision that lifts

one above the clouds where the sweep
of sky is unbroken. There is an ignorance of culture as well as of illiteracy.
One may find ignorance in academic halls
quite as readily as in the haunts of the
day labourer. When you realize the
depths of your own ignorance—the iniquity of race and religious hatreds, social snobbery, and industrial injustice,
you have reached the foothills from
which you may view the heights it is
necessary to climb to get in communion
with true knowledge. Aesculapius re-
storing the sight of the Aristophanic
Plutus, typifies the meaning of education
which is simply the effort to make the
blind see.

It is the ground idea of modern thinkers that the chief aim of existence is
race culture and that progress is an
eternal and an ordered law. When we
walk abroad in the world of Imagination
and Memory, we see everywhere, wrecks
and ruins and pulled-down things; but
through an opening in the trees we may
see the rebuilding in the land of To-
morrow, of things that will be after we
are gone.

Progress, the battle of Today with
Yesterday for the possession of Tomor-
row, operates through two great forces
—Evolution, which is biological or physical; and Suggestion, which is psycho-
logical or mental.

In tracing the biological or physical
history of man, we find that his needs
and his primitive struggles with nature

to gain subsistence, made work a necessity. Through successive ages he gradually gained knowledge, and through Suggestion improved the implements of labour. Hunger made it necessary to get food. The cold suggested shelter and led him to protect his body by a covering, usually of skins, the beginnings of clothing. Primitive man dwelt in trees, in lakes, and in caves. It was a struggle for existence with little idea of co-operation. Every man's hand was raised against his brother and war and bloodshed were the universal rule. Painfully man went through successive stages—the stone age, the age of bronze or metals, etc. Uncounted ages must have passed before the suggestion of soil cultivation came to mankind, and Agriculture gave the first impetus to Civilization.

In the Bible we are told that the first man was named Adam and that he started perfect—sort of armed cap-a-pie for the struggle of life, which in Eden, was no struggle at all until Eve had that apple discussion with the serpent. It was a golden age such as poets, among others the pagan Hesiod, loved to picture. But science pretty conclusively proves that friend Adam might better be called Dennis and surnamed Hathnaught. Far from having fallen from a state of pristine innocence, he is on the ascending scale, working painfully toward the land of better things. It has been a hard journey, and it is a far cry from the fig leaf to the dress suit.

You will find ample evidence of this in Sir John Lubbock's "Prehistoric Times," and "Origin of Civilization"; Drummond's "Ascent of Man"; Darwin's "Origin of Species" and "Descent of Man"; L. H. Morgan's "Ancient Society"; Winwood Reade's "Martyrdom of Man"; the various works of Sir Henry Sumner Maine; Edmund B. Tylor's "Early History of Mankind," and "Primitive Culture"; Frazer's "Golden Bough."

In the view of Science man's progress is upward, and out of an original state of barbarism and savagery, he is working toward culture and the higher life. Briefly, theology holds that man, through the sin of Adam degenerated, and can only be redeemed through the grace of religion. Science holds that barbarism was a stage of evolution or progress and in no sense the result of degeneration.

"Primitive Man" is also ably discussed in a work of that name by Louis Figuier, in which not only is it shown that man harks back to an immense antiquity, but that he has had to fight for every advantage he has gained. He goes into full discussions of the "Stone Age" and the "Age of Metals," and shows man dwelling in caves and hollows, dressed in skins, and limited to a few implements of wood and stone.

Early society originated in the family under the rule of the father or patriarch; an aggregation of families formed the clan or tribe under a chief, and as authority spread, a confederation of tribes became the nation under a King. Authority is designed to establish internal order and external security. It originated in Suggestion and its development has been constantly along the lines of Evolution. In a primitive combat one brute overcomes another, and victory naturally suggests the idea of domination.

All living creatures from ants to man have more or less of the gregarious spirit and gather in communities. In the family relation, however primitive, the authority of the parents is established over the children, and some investigators believe that in the very earliest of times, the family circle constituted a matriarchy, gynecocracy or metrocracy, with the mother supreme over all. As man began to acquire a knowledge of the sex relation and its significance, the father became all powerful and gradually there developed the subjection of woman which still obtains in the world with such force, buttressed as it is with tradition and a so-called religious sanction, that millions of foolish virgins and matrons, gladly subscribing to the convention that they are a weak and inferior lot, become the most venomous opponents of sex equality and Woman's emancipation.

Lawlessness and absence of restraint breed discomfort and insecurity, and authority grew in proportion as the leaders that had won the right to command through brute power and strength of will and mind, gained adherents. It is natural for authority, unrestrained by external forces or internal opposition to drift toward absolutism, and so finally throughout the world the old freedom of the individual will disappeared and tyranny was established with the power of life and death over subjects, vested in the rulers. This tyranny in time took on a kind of sacerdotal function and gradually in men's minds grew a belief in the divinity of Kings and the custom of investing them with power through elaborate and ornate symbolism and ceremony.

Human progress has been greatly advanced by man's efforts to mitigate the miseries of existence. In an age of cold and lack of comfort we may well believe that fire came into the life of man as a great blessing. This will always be associated with the wonderful story of Prometheus. Taking pity on man, Prometheus stole fire from Heaven and gave it to humankind whereupon he incurred the wrath of Zeus, and was condemned to be bound on a rock of the Caucasus with a vulture continually gnawing at his liver. On this myth Aeschylus based his great tragedy of "Prometheus Bound," which is supposed to be the only existing part of a trilogy unfolding the whole story.

Hesiod, who was approximately a contemporary of Homer, also tells the Promethean myth in his "Works and Days," and it will always be to his honour that although he lived in an age when labour was despised, he sang of the dignity of labour.

God himself, we are told in the Bible, indorsed labour when he said that in the sweat of his brow, man should earn his bread.

According to Herodotus, an important business among the Thracians was the sale of their children for exportation. But industry was not held in high repute. Thus: "To be idle is most honourable; but to be a tiller of the soil, most dishonourable; to live by war and rapine most glorious." Handicrafts were little esteemed in those early ages of war and the exploitation of man. Says Herodotus: "Whether the Greeks learned the custom from the Egyptians I am unable to determine with certainty, seeing that the Thracians, Scythians, Persians, Lydians, and almost all barbarous nations hold in less honour than their other citizens, those who learn any art and their descendants, but deem such to be noble as abstain from handicrafts, and particularly those who devote themselves to war. All the Greeks, moreover, have adopted the same notion, and especially the Lacedaemonians; but the Corinthians hold handicraftsmen in least disesteem."

There were many honourable exceptions to this general contempt for labour that characterized the upper classes of antiquity. Everybody is familiar with the story of Cincinnatus, who when called to become dictator of Rome was at the plough, according to Livy. Plutarch in his life of Philopoemen, called "the last of the Greeks," relates that a woman of

Megara, mistaking that distinguished man for a servant desired him to assist her in the business of the kitchen, whereupon he set about to cleave some wood. English story tellers relate a similar tale of King Alfred, with the exception that the Saxon was put to watching cakes to prevent them from burning.

While on his estate Philopoemen slept as one of the labourers and he worked, according to Plutarch, with his vine dressers and ploughmen. Thus, one of the greatest men of his age touched elbows with the humblest, and ennobled labour by example.

Theognis has many a fling at those that toil, and Aristotle had a contempt for labour as a mere manual phase of existence. He held the barbarian to be an inferior breed, born to obey, as the Greek was to command, and assigned him as slave, the duty of doing work with hands, leaving the citizen time for politics, social enjoyment and the pursuit of the beautiful as reflected in art, letters, music, philosophy, and the gymnasium, where he developed symmetry of body. Woman he regarded as merely a race propagator, in every way inferior to man and subject to him.

Aristophanes, to some extent, shared with Aristotle and other ancients, this contempt for labour, for we see him hurling at his enemy Euripides the taunt that his mother had gained a livelihood as an herb woman.

Curiously enough, too, Socrates, as reported by Xenophon in his "Economics," takes largely the same view of woman as a domestic labourer that Aristotle did, although his great disciple Plato, in his "Republic," would elevate her position and improve her education.

In the so-called suffragette comedies of Aristophanes—the Thesmophoriazusœ, the Eccleziazusœ, and the Lysistrata, we find ancient woman's revolt against the intolerable domestic slavery to which custom had condemned her, a demand akin to that of the suffragette of to-day.

Industrial pursuits among the ancients were often hereditary, son following father. In discussing the Spartans or Lacedaemonians, Herodotus says: "In this respect also the Lacedaemonians resemble the Egyptians: their heralds, musicians, and cooks succeed to their fathers' professions; so that a musician is son of a musician, a cook of a cook, and a herald of a herald; nor do others on account of the clearness of their voice apply themselves to this profession and exclude others; but they continue to practice it after their fathers. These things, then, are so."

In this little book, we shall endeavour to trace the history of the Hathnaughts through all its stages—compulsory labour or slavery; serfdom and feudalism; rise of the cities; trade development; crafts; wages; factories; trade-unionism; socialism; syndicalism; feminism—as reflected in the works of historians, philosophers, novelists, economists, poets, of all ages and nations. Naught shall be set down in malice, yet while we hope to receive the benediction of "Imprimatur," there are some we feel that will load us with maledictions and consign us to the common hangman.

CHAPTER II.

DENNIS HATHNAUGHT EARLY AS-
SUMES THE HOD.

Man is essentially a peddler and a trader. Little Stonehatchet Skinclothes, when he could not get what he wanted by force, learned through the suggestion of exchange to "Swap" with his cave and tree dwelling playmates as little Johnny Jones does with the boys of today. The elder Skinclothes dickered and bartered. As time went on and man's necessities grew, the ancients began making trading trips by caravans, camels, pack horses, and small boats, just as the elder Jones now possesses great workshops, fields, golden with plenty, good highways, railroads and steamships to facilitate the business of commerce. From ancient barter has developed modern commerce, and our system of coinage and the conveniences of our banking arrangements are the successors of the articles of exchange, coloured beads, wampum, trinkets, fancy cloths and the innumerable other substitutes of the primitive world for money.

In primitive times labour was, for the most part, compulsory. So remote in the history of the industrial life was the origin of the institution of slavery that surviving annals show no record of its beginning. War made it possible to get slaves easily and their number grew to such proportions that in the time of Sylla there were 13,000,000 of the tribe in Italy alone. We find this statement in the International Encyclopedia. The same authority, taking its facts from pre-existing authorities, tells us that slave labour was first made a systematic business by the Phœnicians, who established a regular trade of buying and selling slaves.

Aristotle, who limited culture to his own ideal—the citizen of a Greek city state—supports the institution of slavery by elaborate argument in his "Politics." He describes a Greek gentleman's family as consisting of man, wife, children and slaves. The position of the wife as defined by Aristotle is far from a happy one. Her main purpose, according to the Stagirite, is to perpetuate the species and to superintend the labour of the slaves and the upbringing of the children. She must submit without question to her husband's commands and could never hope to share in his social or political life. The white slave of to-day, whose wrongs are being so widely discussed, in ancient Greece would really be the only free woman, for the seclusion of married women made it possible only for the courtesans of Greece to share the larger life of the citizens.

We have mentioned the part the Phœnicians have played in the history of slavery. Greatest of the Phœnician colonies was Carthage on the north coast of Africa, which in turn grew to be a powerful state, the rival of Rome and an actual menace to the supremacy of that mistress of the world. Splendid pictures of life in Carthage and the deplorable state of the industrial classes are shown by Gustave Flaubert in his romance of "Salammbo," daughter of Hamilcar and sister of Hannibal.

It was the Phœnicians who developed early industrial life beyond all antiquity. Herodotus, in the opening of his history, tells of their migration from the Red Sea to the Mediterranean and of distant voyages made by their merchants, all of which, we know, tended to the growth of industrial life and increased the demand for labour.

Herodotus has some curious entries on the subject of labour. For example, Tritantæchmes, son of Artabazus, Satrap or governor of Babylon, had so great a number of Indian dogs that four large towns in the plains were exempted from all other taxes so that their inhabitants might find food for the dogs. So you see, milady who neglects human kind and children in her devotion to her lapdog has good ancient precedent in providing her pet with a retinue of servants.

Herodotus tells us that in Egypt, the women attended markets and traffic while the men stayed at home weaving. Men carried burdens on their heads, women on their shoulders. Sons were not compelled to support their parents, but daughters had no choice and were compelled to do so. The wash lady was an important worker, no doubt, for the Egyptians wore linen garments, constantly fresh washed. Men wore two garments, women but one, so we might see the spectacle in an ancient Egyptian substitute for a department store of greater variety in men's goods than in those of women. Linen was an important article of manufacture and of export.

Embalming was an important trade in Ancient Egypt and Herodotus tells some facts about the embalmers that prove their business methods not unlike that of the undertaker of to-day, who shows the bereaved various coffins with prices carefully graded to meet the purses of mourners. When the dead body was brought to the embalmers, they showed the bearers wooden models of corpses made exactly alike by painting. They showed the most expensive manner of embalming, next an inferior kind, and lastly the cheapest of all. There have been tricks in all trades, yea, from the very beginning.

In the time of Cheops, Herodotus says, the wicked king shut up the temples and ordered all the Egyptians to work for him. Some were appointed to draw stones from the quarries in the Arabian mountain down to the Nile; others to receive the stones when transported in vessels across the river and to drag them up the mountain called the Libyan. One hundred thousand men at a time worked in this manner, each party during three months.

"The time," continues Herodotus, "during which the people were thus harassed by toil, lasted ten years on the road which they constructed, along which they drew the stones, a work, in my opinion, not much less than the pyramids, . . . On this road then ten years were expended, and in forming the subterranean apartments on the hill, on which the pyramids stand, which he had made as a burial vault for himself, in an island formed by draining a canal from the Nile." Twenty years were expended in the building of the pyramid itself. Herodotus adds that an interpreter told him a certain inscription on the pyramid explained how much had been expended in radishes, onions, and garlic for the workmen—one thousand six hundred talents of silver. The historian speculates how much more was expended in iron tools, in bread, and in clothes for the labourers.

To provide all these necessities of food and dress would imply that many other thousands of Hathnaughts were engaged in weaving and in working iron, while uncounted other unfortunates made the soil productive of crops, the prosperity of which they could not hope to share with a King so avaricious and egotistical that he drained the labour of the land for twenty years so that his vile and worthless body might have imposing sepulchre at the end of his infamous reign of fifty years. The pyramid-building craze seized his brother Chephren also, and in the course of his fifty-six years of power he, too, exhausted the land. "Thus," says Herodotus, "one hundred and six years are reckoned during which the Egyptians suffered all kinds of calamities."

Blessings returned with Mycerinus, son of Cheops, who "permitted the people, who were worn down to the last extremity, to return to their employments."

With the Scythians, Herodotus says, cattle raising rather than agriculture was the great industry and this was carried on by the labour of the tribe of Hathnaught. The Scythians had a cruel habit of depriving their slaves of sight. In describing their methods of dairy labour he tells of a rude kind of churning: "When they have finished milking, they pour the milk into hollow wooden vessels, and having placed the blind men round about the vessels, they agitate the milk; and having skimmed off that which swims on the surface, they consider it the most valuable, but that which subsides is of less value than the other."

All of which would indicate that butter making is an ancient industry, but we no longer think it necessary to deprive the workers of sight.

It has always been a matter of astonishment to students of man's social history, that great masses of the people should uncomplainingly and servilely submit to oppression. Herodotus tells a story of certain Scythians who, having withdrawn from their country for a period of twenty-eight years, found themselves on their return opposed by a new and vigorous population—young men born of the blind slaves and the wives of the absent Scythians. When they found it impossible to overcome these youths, one of the wiser among the returning Scythians suggested that they throw away their arms and rush upon their opponents with whips, for, he sagely argued, the whip would remind them of their condition of servitude. The Scythians carried out the suggestion, and the youths docilely submitted to be beaten and enslaved. Like the young lackey in Charles Rann Kennedy's "Servant in the House," who was shocked to see his young mistress assist in clearing the table, his ancient prototypes probably "knew their places."

How else can we account for the submission of the Helots, the Hathnaughts of Sparta, who far outnumbered their oppressors? The Langhorns, summarizing ancient testimony, in their translation of Plutarch assert that "these poor wretches were marked out for slaves in their dress, their gestures, and, in short, in everything. They wore dogskin bonnets and sheepskin vests; they were forbidden to learn any liberal art, or to perform any act worthy of their masters. Once a day they received a certain number of stripes for fear they should forget they were slaves, and to crown all, they were liable to the cryptia, which was sure to be executed on all such as spoke, looked, or walked like freemen."

"Perhaps," says Plutarch, "it was the cryptia, as they called it, or ambuscade, if that was really one of this lawgiver's (Lycurgus') institutions, as Aristotle says it was, which gave Plato so bad an impression both of Lycurgus and his laws.

"The governors of the youth ordered the shrewdest of them from time to time to disperse themselves in the country, provided only with daggers and some necessary provisions. In the daytime they hid themselves, and rested in the most private places they could find, but at night they sallied out into the roads, and killed all the Helots they could meet with. Nay, sometimes by day they fell upon them in the fields and murdered the ablest and strongest of them. Thucydides relates in his history of the Peloponnesian war, that the Spartans selected such of them as were distinguished for their courage, to the number of two thousand or more, declared them free, crowned them with garlands and conducted them to the temples of the gods; but soon after they all disappeared; and no one could either then or since give account in what manner they were destroyed.

"Aristotle particularly says the ephori, as soon as they were invested in their office, declared war against the Helots, that they might be massacred under pretense of law. In other respects they treated them with great inhumanity; sometimes they made them drink till they were intoxicated, and in that condition led them into the public halls to show the young men what drunkenness was. They ordered them to sing mean songs, and to dance ridiculous dances, but not to meddle with any that were genteel and graceful. Thus, they tell us that when the Thebans afterwards invaded Laconia and took a great number of the Helots prisoners, they ordered them to sing odes of Terpander, Alcman or Spendon, the Lacedæmonian, but they excused themselves, alleging that it was forbidden by their masters. Those who say that a freeman in Sparta was most a freeman, and a slave most a slave, seem well to have considered the difference of states."

Other authorities take exception to this, declaring that isolated instances of cruelty prove no systematic oppression of the Helots. Thomas Keightley in his once popular school "History of Greece" summarizes all the evidence favourable to the Spartans and declares that the condition of the Helots more resembled that of the villeins of the Middle Ages, or the peasants of Russia, than of slaves in general. But Keightley, venturing the hope that his history might be regarded as a good introduction to Thirlwall's History of Greece, betrays his leanings, for Thirlwall's sympathies are aristocratic, even as those of the abler George Grote are democratic.

In Rome the impatience of the Hathnaughts was always greater than among other nations of antiquity. In Livy, Plutarch and other ancient writers we are entertained with the story of the struggles of the Hathnaughts or plebeians for recognition and share in the government, of the agrarian agitations and of the tumults that resulted in the deaths of Tiberius and Caius Gracchus, champions of the tribe of Hathnaught.

Scholars differ concerning the extent to which the compulsory labour of the Hathnaughts was employed in ancient times. The Encyclopædia Britannica (11th edition) article, "Labour Legislation," declares that there was undoubtedly a certain amount of free labour, even at the time when Egypt was plunged in the craze of pyramid building.

Grote, in his "History of Greece," has an interesting account of the poor free labourers of Greece, and a later authority, William Scott Ferguson, in "Greek Imperialism," maintains that great masses of the free Athenians were forced by circumstances to labour and to take an active part in the trade of the day. This would imply an honourable antiquity for the pay envelope.

Theodor Mommsen, whose "History of Rome" is a work of immense learning despite certain alleged shortcomings on the side of partisanship, takes account of the free labour of ancient Rome. As fresh land was acquired by the state the patrician class claimed to control it, a claim bitterly contested by the Hathnaughts, particularly of the agricultural class. The struggle took the form, he says, of a demand for political rights and resulted in the appointment of tribunes of the Plebs with power of veto. This struggle with privilege lasted two hundred years. An important change was effected by the Canuleian law which made marriage between plebeians and patricians valid. The Licinian law, eighty years later, admitted plebeians to the consulship and required the employment of free labour in agriculture. Gradually there arose a new aristocracy, partly plebeian in origin, but in course of time those new families became as oppressive as the old, for in the time of Tiberius Gracchus the free agricultural class had disappeared and the land had become divided into immense estates, worked by slave labour. Centuries were to pass before this yoke was removed from the necks of the tribe of Hathnaught.

In Rome in the time of Cæsar and Cicero, according to W. Warde Fowler (Social Life at Rome in the Age of Cicero) the poor free plebeian population was housed in great lodging-houses called insulæ or islands because they stood detached and surrounded on all sides by streets just as islands are by water. It is believed there were shops or tabernæ on the first floor, probably bakeries where grain was ground and bread sold cheaply. At times an immense multitude, estimated to have numbered several hundred thousand, received free grain from the government, for it was a favourite way among the ancients, just as it is at present, to allay the discontent of the mob through the stomach. The free workers in leather, shoemaking, clothing and other trades had guilds, perhaps somewhat after the manner of the Trade Unions, but there is no evidence that this free labour ever complained of the competition of slave labour.

With the Romans, conquest and territorial aggrandizement were national passions and in the train of the legions followed the merchant and trader. The Roman genius for road building made the empire a network of magnificent highways and colonies planted at points determined with a masterly grasp of strategical valuations, Romanized the provinces and gradually turned the barbarians into Latin-speaking Roman citizens, proud of the common empire whose expansion they had formerly resisted with immense loss of life and resultant slavery.

From such a system it was natural that commerce should spring, and into the nature of this business scholars are now inquiring with such zeal and success that one need not have much imagination to conjure up some sort of a picture of the teeming Roman world.

Let us take an imaginary journey back to Rome along the road of yesterday under the guidance of Fowler, Abbott's "Common People of Ancient Rome," Herberman's "Business Life in Ancient Rome," Gibbon and Ferrero. We see the shops along the streets with signs and window dressing not unlike the system in vogue in our day. A string of hams in front of a shop indicates the provision store. There are restaurants and inns everywhere, but no chairs at table, for the Roman dined while lounging or reclining.

The street hawker we find as great a nuisance as he is today, finally becoming the subject of state regulation. The travelling cook with apparatus set up in the street sells his steaming sausages, as his latter day brother sells the hot frankfurter.

Our modern merchant would not care for Roman streets; raised stones set at intervals from side to side interfered with the rapid transit of drays and doubtless came in for condemnation from many an ancient board of trade. The object of these stones was to insure the pedestrian dry passage in wet weather, for to the Roman overshoes were unknown.

We find great storage houses and granaries all over Rome, and a thoroughly organized banking system that lent money and undertook the capitalization of all sorts of industries, public works, shipping, and the collecting of taxes, always farmed out to the highest bidder. These bankers and money lenders had their agents throughout the empire. There was a well organized postal service with the mail deliveries expedited by relays of swift horses. Intelligence of state and distant happenings was made known by means of that ancient prototype of the newspaper, the Acta Diurna Romani Populi (Daily Acts of the Roman People), a news service in Cæsar's time posted at important points, something after the manner of a modern newspaper's bulletin board. The news was brought in by couriers, constituting a kind of pony express.

Let us mingle with the crowds about the "Acta." We are surprised at the absence of classic Latin speech and the prevalence of colloquialisms bearing a strange resemblance to our slang, with ancient equivalents of "Do you catch on?" "Gave the old man a touch," etc.

The Roman, no matter how careless his manner of life, was a stickler for a fine funeral and everywhere we find burial associations. There was a great deal of private philanthropy as there is with us, for Rome had its Rockefellers and Carnegies, but no state provision for old age, no workhouses for the indigent poor, no hospitals to relieve the suffering.

Property was held at private risk, for there was no system of insurance, yet arson was common and men often destroyed their own homes. It was the custom of the Roman after a fire to give the victim goods and money, and often such private contributions amounted to more than the loss. This might be regarded as a species of insurance and explains the temptation "to make a fire" which is still common in the modern world.

We discover in ancient trade combinations the ancestor of the octopus or modern trust. Manufacturing was largely carried on under the domestic system, the workers, free or slave, being employed at home rather than gathered in great factories as with us. The minute sub-division of labour is traceable to the Roman passion for system, efficiency and organization. There were not only 250 different divisions of slaves, but free labour was organized according to the handicraft of the worker. These guilds of free workmen, so far as research goes to show, did not combine to raise wages and lower working hours, but to gain through the fraternal spirit comradeship and improved social life. The guilds had their rituals, and their officers and insignia were patterned after the titles and insignia of the Roman government officials.

In the next chapter we shall deal specifically with the question of slavery, the most important of all, for the brunt of Rome's industrial battle fell to the lot of the empire's beasts of burden, the unrequited toilers.

CHAPTER III.

DENNIS' IRON COLLAR—"SERVUS SUM."

In the preceding chapter it has been shown that the tribe of Hathnaught was very numerous in the Roman World. In time, the tribe became distinguished by a peculiar mark of ignobility—an iron collar worn about the neck on which was the inscription—"Servus Sum"—I am a slave. Added to this was the name of the gentleman or lady that revelled in luxury at the expense of the un-requited toil of the Hathnaughts. The tribe worked from daylight to darkness, faring on scant rations and always liable to the most horrible punishments and chastisements. Mere whim at any time could send a slave to the torture cham-ber. He could not give testimony in a Court of law except under the torture. When his master offered him as a wit-ness, he was put to "the question" and it often resulted in death.

Juvenal, greatest of all the satirists that the world has ever known, tells us that some of the grand Roman dames used to keep paid torturers and that while their hair was being dressed, they amused themselves listening to the sound of the lash and the cries of the poor victims who had been stripped for punishment so that a degenerate yearning to witness human suffering might be satisfied.

Gibbon in his "Decline and Fall of the Roman Empire" has many pictures drawn from the annals of the House of Hathnaught, but Gibbon lacked the sublime indignation that surged in the Juvenalian soul, and his words lack the passion of resentment.

In the camp of Lucullus, he tells us, an ox sold for a drachma, a Hathnaught for four drachmas or about three shillings. "The slaves," he says, "consisted for the most part of barbarian captives, taken in thousands by the chances of war, purchased at a vile price (just quoted), accustomed to a life of independence, and impatient to break and to avenge their fetters."

It was long before the protection of the law was extended to the slaves and mitigated, in a measure, the severity of the masters, but manumission was not encouraged too freely even in the best of times, through the fear that newly acquired freedom for multitudes of bondmen might set loose a dangerous element that was bound to the empire by no tie of blood, kinship, or nationality.

Freedmen, Gibbon says, were excluded from civil or military honours, and the stigma of servile origin clung to them for three or four generations. Many of the slaves were men of learning—physicians and philosophers—and often a noble Roman possessed hundreds or even thousands of bondmen. That their lives were lightly valued is shown by the story of Pedanius Secundus. The four hundred slaves under his roof were all put to death for not preventing his murder.

Almost every profession, either liberal or mechanical, might be found in the household of an opulent Senator, Gibbon says, and in the International Encyclopedia we find it stated that in Rome there were as many as two hundred and fifty different classes of slaves. Public slaves were the property of the State, and were engaged in road building and other public works. The private slaves, we read in the Encyclopaedia Britannica, were divided into two kinds—familia rustica or rural, and familia urbana or domestic. Over the rural slaves was the villicus, a chief slave or overseer. They worked in chain gangs, and at night, according to Wallon's "History of Slavery," were confined in the ergastulum or underground slave prison.

According to Gibbon the Hathnaughts were at least equal in number to the free inhabitants of the Roman world.

An historian of our own times, Guglielmo Ferrero, goes deeper than Gibbon into the origin of the Roman slave trade—the exploitation of members of the tribe of Hathnaught for the enrichment of pre-Christian seigniors. It is the opinion of Ferrero (Greatness and Decline of Rome) that this trade had its beginning in the scarcity of the old free labour and the disinclination of free workmen to engage in tasks that promised a bare living and no assured future of improved personal conditions.

Lester F. Ward, author of "Pure Sociology," appears to have had a similar thought in mind when, noting the disinclination of the Hathnaughts to labour, he says: "How did man learn to work? Did the needs of existence teach him self-denial, tone down his wild, unsettled nature, and discipline his mind and body to daily toil? Not at all. It is safe to say that if left wholly to these influences man would have never learned to labour. It required some other influence far more imperative and coercive. In a word, nothing short of slavery could ever have accomplished this. This was the social mission of human slavery—to convert mere activity into true labour."

Whatever the cause, Ferrero shows that in the second century before Christ there was established in Rome a vast and systematized traffic in the flesh of the Hathnaughts. Traders followed the armies and bought the prisoners who were promptly resold to the best advantage to their masters. Kings of Numidia and Mauritania even sold their own subjects in their eagerness for gain. Caravans of slaves poured into Rome from Gaul, Germany, and the East. The Hathnaughts were sold without regard to their feelings or family ties, wherever it pleased the dealers to send them. All that was expected of them was submission and labour. In some instances those that showed special aptitude were educated in various arts and were even made proficient with the sword with a view of being hired out by their masters as gladiators at great funerals.

In "Quo Vadis," "Fabiola," and like books we get fine pictures of the slaves —pictures that are redolent of the life of antiquity. We see the unpaid and ill-treated Hathnaughts dancing attendance on the great whom some one has estimated to number not more than thirty thousand in an empire teeming with millions of humankind. We find Dennis and his wife and children attending their masters and mistresses at the toilet, in the bath, at the table, and in the kitchen. They had to furnish the idlers with amusement and entertainment, no matter how heavy of heart they might be. When the great ventured abroad, the handsomest of the tribe of Hathnaught attended them. Dennis had no day off and no vacation. Perquisites he picked up here and there were called his "peculium" and often these tips formed the nucleus of the fund that eventually purchased his freedom.

To the everlasting credit of the tribe, be it said, they were not altogether contented to wear the collar of servitude. One of the house, Spartacus Hathnaught, roused the enslaved population in 73 B. C. and engaged in a great servile insurrection which was successfully waged by the slaves armed with all sorts of weapons, until the superior discipline and resources of the Romans conquered. With the death of Spartacus, the Hathnaughts' insurrection was at an end and the tribe resumed its shackles.

These shackles were not broken until Christianity became firmly established in the empire which soon afterward fell, and slavery was replaced by that later form of servitude known as the feudal system. By that time the rural slaves of Rome had become merged in the class of the coloni. The colonus in the old days of Rome was a freeman who worked a farm sometimes under lease and sometimes under a form of metayage.

CHAPTER IV.

THE WORLD'S MIDNIGHT—HATH-NAUGHT AS SERF.

Knowledge of the history of the Middle Ages. is necessary if we would trace in order, the annals of the house of Hathnaught. Edward Everett rightly called the period, "the midnight of the world."

Victor Duruy's sweeping view has the advantage of brevity. Particularly good is his account of feudalism. William Robertson has viewed the period in an introductory volume to his "History of Charles, the Fifth," and Henry Hallam's work on the subject is still widely read and studied, although later research has led scholars to question certain of his conclusions and to bring the charge of inaccuracy against him. No one, however, has ever impugned his sincerity or charged him with partiality—the curse of the special advocate in historical writing.

J. F. C. Hecker's "Epidemics of the Middle Ages," a German work of which there is a translation by B. C. Babington, contains a mass of matter about "The Black Death" of the fourteenth century and that mysterious scourge of the race, "the Sweating Sickness" which came in five successive periods, the last in 1551. The "Black Death" swept away 25,-000,000 of Europe's inhabitants and it is said that in one cemetery near London, 50,000 bodies were buried.

The world's midnight began in 476 A. D. when the triumph of Odoacer in Italy put an end to the Roman Empire. It lasted until the Turks took Constantinople in 1453 and the Ottoman power supplanted that of the Eastern empire. The Dark Ages, when intellect was in eclipse, are usually held to include the period from the time of Odoacer until the thirteenth century when there was such a notable revival of intellectual activity along all lines that Dr. James Walsh has characterized it as the greatest of the centuries.

The Middle Ages, so far as the mass of the people counted, constituted one thousand years of darkness, crime, degradation, superstition and injustice. Here and there a scholar, usually a monk, kept the candle of progress burning while he busied himself with research, experiment, or the copying of manuscripts, but the ruling powers, the nobility and churchmen, cared little save for the perpetuation of their own power.

The church opposed the feudal system, not because it oppressed the serfs, but because it divided the serf's allegiance and deprived the ecclesiastical power of supreme domination by making the serf directly dependent upon his overlord.

Feudalism, according to Duruy, was first recognized by the edict of Kierry-sur-Oise (877) whereby Charles the Bald recognized the right of a son to inherit the fief or the office of his father.

Under the feudal system everybody became somebody's man. The great seignior was the vassal of the king; the seigniors in turn parcelled out the land to their own vassals in return for military and other services. The vassal was obliged to enroll for war under his lord and to supply him with money—first to ransom him in the event of captivity; second to defray the expenses incident to the knighting of the seignior's or lord's eldest son; third, to provide a dowry for the lord's daughter. These contributions were called aides. The vassal did homage to his lord and through an act of homage, sons of vassals on the death of their fathers, received in turn their lands from feudal lords. Often there was a symbolic offering from vassal to lord, of a sod or other trifle in acknowledgment of his overlordship.

There was a marked difference between the feudalism of France and that which obtained in England. In France subinfeudation was practiced to such an extent that, as Buckle remarks, oppression became an organized system. The vassal who held his land from the overlord, let it out to others responsible to himself, while these in turn subdivided the land until the lowest man had masters running back by the score. In England, in the time of the first Edward, the statute known as Quia Emptors forbade subinfeudation and lessened the load of the Hathnaughts. To this day in France the effect of subinfeudation is seen in the intensive agriculture of the peasantry on small plots of ground.

The mass of the population during the Middle Ages, were serfs attached to their particular estate or glebe without hope of emancipation and debarred by cruel penalties from ever leaving it. Lords through their bailiffs and serf-masters held the Hathnaughts in check and were at liberty to treat them as they pleased, and more often than not it pleased them to submit them to outrage and cruel exactions.

If a girl serf happened to be pretty she was at the mercy of her master without right of appeal or redress, and if she were to marry, her lord could at will take the bridegroom's place the first night. This was called the "right of first fruits", "Droit du Seignior", or "Jus primae Noctis" (law of the first night), and is described with terrible realism in Eugene Sue's "Mysteries of the People." The law is also worked into the plot of Beaumarchais' comedy of Figaro.

The Encyclopædia Britannica (11th edition), says there is no trustworthy evidence that the law ever had official sanction but admits that lawless barons very likely enforced it. John Lothrop Motley (Rise of the Dutch Republic), holds that there was such a law, which led Bismarck to take issue with him, contending that it was only a tax or money payment exacted by the lord from the bridegroom.

The history of the Hathnaughts in the Middle Ages is realistically pictured by Eugene Bonnemere, in his "Histoire des Paysans." He deals primarily with the period between 1200 and 1850, but in an introduction he traces the history from 50 B. C. to 1200 A. D. In telling the painful story of the French Hathnaughts Bonnemere considers his relation to the nobility and the king and the means whereby an arrogant nobility was able to reduce the French peasants to a state of serfdom, worse than obtained in any other country.

Like Buckle and other authorities he shows that in England to win over the common people to their cause, the nobility had to make concessions to Dennis and let him share in a measure, privilleges the great lords had obtained from the king. In France the nobles were more powerful and could afford to disdain Dennis, who year by year descended more and more into the scale of serfdom while in England the people were gaining slowly, but surely, point after point, and gradually building up that glorious unwritten charter, the British Constitution.

Magna Charta was wrested from King John at Runnymede in June, 1215, and greatly extended popular rights and privileges. In 1264 English cities were returning members to Parliament and the House of Commons came into existence and began that fight with Privilege that has only ended in our day by the Commons winning supremacy over the House of Lords.

Feudalism like slavery had its useful as well as its dark side. It established authority and built up population by fixing man in a set abode. But the authority being irresponsible, became a tyranny that proved its own undoing and eventually led to its fall.

To the Middle Ages we owe other remarkable institutions—Monasticism, the Crusades, Chivalry, and trial by ordeal.

Monasticism had its origin in the desire of the soul-weary to find a refuge from a world full of injustice and turmoil. In the seclusion of the monasteries the monks copied and illuminated manuscripts, thus saving to mankind the priceless gift of learning, particularly of classical Greek and Roman literature. Out of the monastic school often developed the University. Monastic example improved farming methods and by dignifying manual labour, taught respect for work.

Monks were not only the manufacturers and educators, but took care of the sick and orphans and developed the idea of service that we see to-day in our great hospitals. The abuse of the monastic life was that it withdrew the best men and women from a world that could illy spare them.

It was a monk, Peter, the Hermit. whose preaching brought on the Crusades, movements that dispatched immense numbers to the East to rescue the Holy Sepulcher from the Saracenic infidels, and which are often described as outbursts of ignorant and fanatical zeal. Yet we must not overlook certain important and enduring effects of these wildly romantic expeditions. They weakened feudalism in its backbone by luring serfs from the soil; they opened up new avenues of commerce and lastly, by disturbing the flow of culture at its eastern fountain head in Constantinople, caused many artists to immigrate to Italy and Germany and thus sent a shaft of light through the Dark Ages.

Chivalry had its origin in the Crusades and in the romantic literature that this coming together of the West and the East brought into existence. It was the old Germanic idea of the sacredness of womanhood, described by Tacitus, brought to full flower by the new military order of knighthood. Only those of noble birth might aspire to be knights, and the candidate for knightly honours was invested with his rank only after a ceremonial that included fasting and prayer, the vigil over his arms, and vows to uphold ideals of honour and humanity. He always selected a lady, often imaginary, as his ideal, and roamed the world in quest of adventure. The joust and tournament were the favourite pastimes and he put all the more ardour into his work from the fact that his lady love was a spectator. To Chivalry is traced the origin of duelling.

Despite the romance that has made the Age of Chivalry glow with life and beauty, we are too often disillusioned by instances of wife-beating and injustice on the part of knights, and Cervantes may be said to have put the world forever in his debt by destroying the institution through Don Quixote.

Perhaps the most terrible of all peculiarities of the Middle Ages was the method of punishment. In H. C. Lea's "History of the Inquisition" we are told that the "wheel, the cauldron of boiling oil, burning alive, burying alive, flaying alive, tearing apart with wild horses, were the ordinary expedients by which the criminal jurist sought to deter crime by frightful examples which would make a profound impression on a not over-sensitive population."

Trial by ordeal proves the amazing prevalence of superstition and ignorance. The usual forms such trials took were the ordeals of fire, water, and personal combat. A person accused might be blindfolded and forced to walk between two fires. If only scorched in slight degree it was held that innocence was established. Again an accused person might be required to walk barefooted on red hot iron and if no burning resulted, innocence was miraculously proved. In the "Lives of the Saints," you may read of a pious royal lady who, without raising so much as a blister, walked upon red hot ploughshares. But the miracle never happened. If it did, precautions were taken to protect the lady's feet. It is a story for the marines.

The water cure for crimes took various forms. If the accused, thrown into water, sank, he was supposed to be innocent, for the act of floating was interpreted to mean that the water wished to eject the guilty, sin-red individual. Persons accused of witchcraft were subjected to this test. In the ordeal of hot water, the accused was required to take a stone out of a boiling cauldron. In some cases one had to plunge the arm as far as the elbow in the boiling water. If the hand and arm readily healed it was proof of innocence.

In the ordeal of personal combat or the wager of battle, the challenger stood facing the west, the person challenged the east. Defeat of the challenged party meant innocence of the accused. In case the vanquished begged for life he was often granted his wish, upon retracting his accusation, and thereafter was known as a recreant.

Trial by ordeal is found to be common up to the thirteenth century and rarer from that time on, as more enlightened councils prevailed and saner ideas of jurisprudence were established. Among primitive peoples it persists to our day, particularly in Africa as we know on the strength of testimony submitted by the great missionary, David Livingstone.

"But did the Middle Ages wholly die?" asks Duruy, who answers his own question: "They bequeathed to Modern Times virile maxims of public and individual rights, which then profited only the lords, but which now profit all. The Middle Ages developed chivalrous ideas, a sentiment of honour, a respect for woman which still stamp with a peculiar seal those who preserve and practice them. Lastly, mediæval architecture remains the most imposing material manifestation of the religious sentiment, an architecture we can only copy when we wish to erect the fittest houses of prayer."

Duruy might have added that in these so-called Dark Ages were founded most of the great schools and universities of Europe and that to these times we owe many great discoveries and inventions of which the most glorious were the discovery of America and the invention of printing.

CHAPTER V.

WHEN DENNIS HATHNAUGHT WAS A SAXON.

In the days of the Anglo-Saxons there were, throughout England, Village Communities, conducted under the Manorial system. The Lord of the Manor was the great man of the community, and under him and attached to the soil were the freemen and villeins. Villeins, who were of the tribe of Hathnaughts, were in a state of serfdom, bound for life to the estate upon which they were born, and under obligations to the Lord of the Manor to render him services in return for his protection and the use of the land. Mainly the services consisted in military duties and agricultural labour. There was little to recommend the condition of the Hathnaughts in Anglo-Saxon days, in comparison with the condition of Sambo Hathnaught, the black slave of Dixie. The Lord of the Manor earned his luxuries in the sweat of his serf's face, and the Anglo-Saxon Dennis always laboured in fear of the lash. As the serf of that day was called Nativus it is believed by some authorities that the mass of the subjugated people were of the displaced Celtic race.

England as it was then, was divided into shires; these again were divided into smaller districts called hundreds and these hundreds into still smaller sub-divisions called tithings.

Hallam in his "Middle Ages," discussing Anglo-Saxon times in England says: "There were but two denominations of persons above the class of servitude, thanes and ceorls; the owners and the cultivators of land, or rather, perhaps, as a more accurate distinction, the gentry and the inferior people. Among all the Northern Nations as is well known, the weregild or composition for murder, was the standard measure of the gradation of society. In the Anglo-Saxon laws, we find two ranks of freeholders; the first called King's thanes whose lives were valued at 1200 shillings; the second of inferior degree, whose composition was half that sum. That of a ceorl was 200 shillings. By the laws of William the Conqueror there was still a composition fixed for the murder of a villein or ceorl, the strongest proof of his being, as it was called law-worthy, and possessing a rank however subordinate in political society. And this composition was due to his kindred, not to the lord. Indeed, it seems positively declared in another passage that the cultivators though bound to remain upon the land were only subject to certain services. Nobody can doubt that the villeini and bordarii of Doomsday Book, who are always distinguished from the serfs of the demesne, were the ceorls of Anglo-Saxon law."

To possess land was the only way to power, social or political. It is believed that to each hundred warriors among the Saxons, a particular portion of land was allotted, and these again divided the land among the different families. Land that remained over was called the folk-land and the king could not grant any of this away without permission of the Witanagemot. Society became divided into Hathnaughts who had no standing in law and were at the mercy of the master; the landless freeman who placed himself in a position of dependence and thus acquired protection under the law; the full freeman who owned land and gauged his rank according to the number of hides of land he owned. The ceorl owned one hide, the thegn or thane, five, and the earl, forty hides. These last classes were on something of an equal footing and one might pass from one to the other with growing wealth.

To Anglo-Saxon days are traced those beginnings of constitutional and ordered government now so general throughout the world. Towns grew by the accidental fact of the proximity of farms and an official called the reeve, attended by four townsmen represented a township's interests in the courts of the Hundred and the Shire. The Hundred was a combination of towns, the gemot or court of the hundred held monthly sessions, and these were attended by the lords of the domains included in the hundred; the reeves and their four men; and the priest of the parish.

Criminals were tried in the Courts of the Hundred and land and other questions decided, usually by twelve men chosen from representatives at the Court. Matters always had to take orderly procedure and it was not legal to hear questions in superior courts until they had first been heard in the Court of the Hundred. An aggregation of Hundreds made up the Shire of which the great man was the earldorman whose office became hereditary and who later became known by the title of earl. The king was represented in the Shire by the sheriff, who convoked, semi-annually, the Shire-moot, or court above the Hundred, and presided over its deliberations, with the earldorman and bishop sitting with him.

Supreme over all was the great council of the nation, the Witanagemot. This must not be confounded with present representative bodies called Parliament and Congress. Its membership was made up of the earldormen, bishops, abbots and thanes. The Witanagemot was not only the Supreme Court of the Anglo-Saxon world, but it had the power of electing the king and promulgating laws. The power of the Witanagemot was of a more or less fluctuating character for a king who was a real king and not a mere figurehead could always bring the Witanagemot to his way of thinking and doing.

Kingly power was largely increased by making the interests of members of his household identical with those of royalty. Gesiths or companions of the king formed a sort of Swiss Guard of royalty, but the gesithcund as time went on disappeared into the general body of thanehood. Thanes became powerful through grants of land from the king and often such grants carried with them power of sac and soc, and in this way, the right of the thane to decide out of hand, matters that in earlier days were submitted to the hundred-moot.

Sac and soc are also written sake and soke. The first involved a cause in dispute between litigants and the right to hold court and administer justice within a specified district. Under the Normans such power was vested in the Manorial Courts. The system in one form or another has been exercised by the Squirearchy of England almost to our own day. Soc or soke as defined by Webster, concerned "the right to hold court and do justice, with the franchise to receive certain fees or fines arising from it; jurisdiction over a certain territory or over certain men, or the right to exercise such jurisdiction or receive certain fees or fines belonging to that right or the territory over which the jurisdiction exists."

Although the king reserved to himself the right of soc or soke over thanes, the tendency of the system was to increase more and more the power of the thanes until in time a few powerful nobles became a menace to royalty as the fountain head of a central authority. In thanehood, Green (History of the English People) found the germ of feudalism. This system indeed did form the raw material of the feudalism introduced so ruthlessly by William the Conqueror, who, with his Normans conquered England in 1066.

Duruy (History of the Middle Ages) with his usual power of presenting vivid pictures of olden times without unnecessary circumlocution describes the manner in which William divided the Saxon lands among his followers.

"The secular and the ecclesiastical domains of the Saxons," he says, "were occupied by the conquerors, many of whom had been cowherds or weavers or simple priests on the continent, but now became lords and bishops. Between 1080 and 1086 a register of all the properties occupied was drawn up. This is the famous land roll of England called by the Saxons the Doomsday Book. On this land thus divided was established the most regular feudal system in Europe. Six hundred barons had beneath them 60,-000 knights. Over all towered the king, who appropriated 1462 manors and the principal cities and by exacting the direct oath from even the humblest knights, attached every vassal closely to himself."

William was wise in his day and generation, and had closely observed, not only the lessening of the royal power in France in consequence of the rise of great feudatories, but the gradual development of a similar system in England as a result of the growth of thanehood. When he granted one of his lords a vast amount of land he took pains to see that the tracts were in widely separated districts, and in this way foiled the ambition of a powerful vassal who might seek to become great in his home Shire.

When England was harassed by the Danes, the Anglo-Saxons were subjected to what is known as the Danegeld, a tribute paid to the piratic Danes. The tax fell upon land under cultivation. William saw fit to continue this tax, and eighteen years after the Conquest tripled it. It was one of the most vexatious exactions that oppressed the Hathnaughts. Another of his oppressive measures was to take over jurisdiction of the forests, and to visit with heavy penalties, even deprivation of sight and life, the presumption of those who dared to kill game therein. This right belonged exclusively to himself and his favourites.

These forest laws led to the outlawry of many persons, and in the old ballads and tales we find stories of the hardy bands that defied the Norman kings, particularly of the romantic deeds of Robin Hood, Little John, Maid Marion and others who found refuge in Sherwood Forest and founded in the greenwood and the brush, the outlaw republic of the Hathnaughts.

Edward Augustus Freeman (History of the Norman Conquest of England) writing of the misfortunes that had come upon the Anglo-Saxons with the death of their King Harold at the Battle of Hastings, declares that from that day the Normans "began to work the will of God upon the folk of England till there were left in England no chiefs of the land of English blood, till all were brought down to bondage and sorrow, till it was a shame to be called an Englishman, and the men of England were no more a people."

The Normans despoiled the Saxon Hathnaughts of everything and exploited the whole land for the conquering race. No more interesting picture of this contest exists in literature than that drawn by Sir Walter Scott in the first chapter of "Ivanhoe." In this we are carried back to the England of Richard the First and in the talk between Wamba the jester and Gurth, the swineherd, we get a graphic picture of the times. Gurth, who is of the house of Hathnaught, bears about his neck a brass band welded on and with the inscription upon it: "Gurth, the son of Beowulph is the born thrall of Cedric of Rotherwood." Wamba shows that everything worth while is given a Norman name, while all that is mean remains Saxon.

"Why, how call you these grunting brutes running about on their four legs?" demanded Wamba.

"Swine, fool, swine," said the herd, "every fool knows that."

"And swine is good Saxon," said the jester, "but how call you the sow when she is flayed and drawn and quartered, and hung up by the heels like a traitor?"

"Pork," answered the swineherd.

"I am very glad every fool knows that too," said Wamba, "and pork, I think is good Norman-French; and so when the brute lives and is in charge of a Saxon slave, she goes by her Saxon name; but becomes a Norman and is called pork, when she is carried to the castle-hall to feast among the nobles; what dost thou think of this, friend Gurth, ha?"

All of which goes to show that friend Wamba, in his way, was as much a walking delegate of sedition as Rousseau ever was. Suggestion is a great teacher.

At the time of the Norman Conquest there was a Saxon slave trade in England, according to Green, Hallam, Taine and other authorities, which had its headquarters at Bristol and was finally suppressed by William the Conqueror. Taine (History of English Literature) tells the story thus: "At Bristol, at the time of the Conquest, as we are told by an historian of the time (Life of Bishop Wolston) it was the custom to buy men and women in all parts of England, and to carry them to Ireland for sale in order to make money. The buyer usually made the young women pregnant, and took them to market in that condition in order to insure a better price." Taine quotes his authority as follows: "You might have seen with sorrow long files of young people of both sexes and of the greatest beauty, bound with ropes, and daily exposed for sale. . . . They sold in this manner as slaves their nearest relative, and even their own children."

Green declares that when Henry II finally undertook the Conquest of Ireland, that country was filled with Saxon Hathnaughts who had been enslaved, and that this was one of the grounds for the invasion. Hallam quotes Giraldus Cambrensis to show that the Irish entered into an agreement, finally, to emancipate the slaves, but he does not name the Hibernian Lincoln of the occasion.

Green ("History of the English People") calls attention to the rise of the universities as a menace to the perpetuity of feudalism. The democratic tendencies of the great Schools did much to undermine the system just as we see in the Russian literature of our own day that the student life in the university towns of Muscovy has hastened the day of Ivan Hathnaught's emancipation and has brought greater freedom to those that toil.

According to Green the university was a protest against the isolation of man from man. With the Latin the tongue of the learned everywhere, "a common intellectual kinship and rivalry," says Green, "took the place of the petty strifes which parted province from province and realm from realm."

Wandering Oxford Scholars carried the writings of Wyclif to the libraries of Prague, we are told, and who can doubt that the interchange of knowledge by different countries hastened the great spiritual revolution of which the English Wyclif and the Bohemian Huss and Jerome of Prague were the precursors—the Reformation of Luther?

CHAPTER VI.

THE BLACK DEATH EMANCIPATES DENNIS.

The Black Death which swept away 25,000,000 of Europe's inhabitants, scourged the Continent between 1348 and 1351. It swept England in 1349. This great calamity had an important bearing on the question of wages and constitutes an epoch in the history of the tribe of Hathnaught.

Says the International Encyclopedia: "The institution of the Guild was the protest of the labouring class against feudalism. Originating in the Anglo-Saxon family system, it became intrenched behind the growing strength of Christianity, and gradually assimilated with it all the forces that were inimical to the control of the labouring class by the feudal barons and other potentates. Through the influence of the Guild, hand-labour became a power, hand labourers were artists, and the golden age of manual skill arrived. In the work of the loom, in metal working and wood carving, in the manufacture of pottery and glass, this period has never been equalled. Artists like the Della Robbias, Ghiberta, Andrea del Sarto, and Benvenuto Cellini ennobled labour. But the age became luxurious, and the masterpieces of art labour centered in a few hands.

"As has ever been the case in history, interests conflicted, wealth tended to centralize and consolidate itself, the Guilds divided among themselves into plodders and those who accumulated the results of their toil, vast operations in trade became possible to those who possessed the necessary enterprise and skill, and so Capital was born as a new factor in the utilization of labour, and a new enemy for the labourer to confront and to antagonize. The influence of the new force was speedily felt, and the tendency to exclusiveness and monopoly on the part of the wealthy awakened in the workers the idea of organization, and there grew up an independent working class for the first time in history. Now, too, for the first time in its application to large and organized bodies of labourers, the wage question took prominence.

"This arose primarily from the effect upon the population of the terrible plagues and famines which, beginning about the middle of the fourteenth century, began to devastate Europe. The depopulation of countries resulted in a scarcity of labourers, but every attempt on the part of the latter to insure the adoption of a higher rate of wages on this account met with strenuous and persistent opposition from employers."

Edgar Sanderson in his "History of the

World," says: "The effect in England (of
the Black Death) was to raise the wages
paid by landowners, who now tilled their
lands mostly by hired labour, and to
cause some legislation to compel the peasants to work at fixed wages in their
own localities. Much of the land ceased,
from the lack of labourers, to be tilled for
corn, and became pasture for the raising
of wool, which was a source of great
profit by export for weaving in the looms
of the Netherlands."

Green (History of the English People)
says: "The social strife, too, gathered bit-
terness with every effort at repression.
It was in vain that Parliament after Parliament increased the severity of its laws.
The demands of the Parliament of 1376
show how inoperative the previous Statutes of Labourers had proved. They
prayed that constables be directed to ar-
rest all who infringed the statute, that no
labourer should be allowed to take refuge
in a town and become an artisan if there
were need of his services in the country
from which he came, and that the king
would protect lords and employers against
the threats of death uttered by serfs
who refused to serve.

"The reply of the Royal Council shows
that statesmen at any rate were beginning to feel that oppression might be
pushed too far. The king refused to interfere by any further and harsher provisions between employers and employed,
and left cases of breach of law to be dealt
with in his ordinary courts of justice—

on the one side he forbade the threatening gatherings which were already common in the country, but on the other he forbade the illegal exactions of the employers. With such a reply, however, the proprietary class were hardly likely to be content. Two years later the Parliament of Gloucester called for a fugitive slave law which would enable lords to seize their serfs in whatever county or town they found refuge, and in 1379 they prayed that judges might be sent five times a year into every shire to enforce the Statute of Labourers."

Frederick W. Hackwood in a work bearing the sarcastic title, "The Good Old Times," also points out the ultimate benefits to Dennis, that followed in the wake of the Black Death. He shows that in consequence of the great mortality, food was cheap and abundant in the first year of the plague.

As the plague continued, agriculture was neglected and the price of food increased enormously. The scarcity of labour put a premium upon it and Dennis was not slow to demand high wages. Hackwood says that the laws aimed at regulating wages and the labour market, were enforced upon the Hathnaughts by fines and punishment of a corporal nature. But it was all to no purpose for a rise in the price of corn made it impossible for Dennis to live under the old wage standard.

Great landowners tried to enforce the regulations of the statute, however, and the expedient was hit upon of branding runaway Hathnaughts on the forehead. Citizens of towns harbouring runaways were liable to severe punishment. Here and there a landowner converted his land into sheep pastures because of the difficulty of getting labour, while others began leasing the land for rental to farmers which put the burden of finding labour to till the soil squarely upon the tenant. Thus originated in the days immediately following the Black Death, the class of tenant farmers now so important an element in rural life—the yeomanry of Merrie England.

Experiments with sheep farming, according to Hackwood, led to important results. The wool trade grew to be a source of great wealth and lords who so employed their land, began to encroach upon the common lands, which they fenced in, thereby arbitrarily and illegally shutting out the Hathnaughts who had long enjoyed the right of free pasturage. It is from this time that date the hedges, so characteristic to-day of the English landscape—a thing of beauty that had its origin in robbery and injustice, and in many instances of tragic results to the long-suffering Hathnaughts.

While these rapacious lords were trying to abolish wages and restore the serfdom of the old feudal days, others of a more discerning kind concluded it would be wiser and in the end more profitable to control all means of supply and make their own bargain with Dennis. Public lands were appropriated by the wholesale by these mediæval land grabbers who pretended a philanthropic desire to reclaim waste places and thus improve the national prosperity. Parliament worked hand in glove with the land robbers and the system continued until 1845 when a million acres were enclosed. Thousands of private acts of Parliament sanctioned this wholesale larceny of the public domain which crowded the Hathnaughts into tighter and tighter quarters on the "tight little island."

John Ball, who preached sedition in the reign of Richard II (1381), inculcated levelling principles among the Hathnaughts, according to David Hume in his "History of England." Says Hume: "The first faint dawn of the arts and of good government in that age, had excited the minds of the populace in different states of Europe, to wish for a better condition, and to murmur against those chains which the laws enacted by the haughty nobility and gentry had so long imposed upon them. The commotions of the people in Flanders, the mutiny of the peasants in France, were the natural effects of the growing spirit of independence; and the report of these events being brought into England, whose personal slavery, **as we** learn from Froissart, was more general than in any other country in Europe, had prepared the minds of the multitude for an insurrection.

"One John Ball, also, a seditious

preacher who affected low popularity, went about the country and inculcated on his audience the principles of the first origin of mankind from one common stock, their equal right to liberty and to all the goods of nature, the tyranny of artificial distinctions and the abuses which had arisen from the degradation of the more considerable part of the species, and the aggrandizement of a few insolent rulers. These doctrines, so agreeable to the populace and so conformable to the ideas of primitive equality which are ingraven in the hearts of all men, were greedily received by the multitude and scattered the sparks of that sedition which the present tax raised into a conflagration."

In a footnote Hume says: "There were two verses at that time in the mouths of the common people, which, in spite of prejudice, one cannot but regard with some degree of approbation:

When Adam delved and Eve span,
Where was then the gentleman?"

The tax mentioned by Hume was the imposition of three groats a head on every person, male or female, above fifteen years of age. The first disorder was raised by a blacksmith of the tribe of Hathnaught, in a village of Essex. The collecting of the tax had been farmed out to tax-gatherers in each county, and one of these insisting on payment for a daughter of the blacksmith, offered indignities to the child with the result that Hathnaught brained him with a hammer.

Immediately the other Hathnaughts rushed to arms headed by Wat Tyler, Jack Straw, Hob Carter, and Tom Miller. One hundred thousand of them assembled at Blackheath, and some of them, to show their purpose of levelling all mankind, forced kisses on the king's mother who was returning from a pilgrimage to Canterbury. Lawyers fared badly, for the Hathnaughts, regarding the men of law as enemies, hanged every one they encountered. Ability to read and write was enough to condemn the victim.

Richard II took refuge in the Tower, but finally had to come forth and deal with the rebels who had been engaged in a campaign of murder and pillage. At a conference with the king, Wat Tyler was so insolent that Walworth, the Mayor of London, struck him down with his sword and members of the king's retinue dispatched the rebel chief. The Hathnaughts would have wreaked a terrible revenge had it not been for Richard's presence of mind. With wonderful coolness he ventured among them and said he would be their leader. The poor simpletons were granted charters and liberties, and they thought the millennium well under way, but not long afterward the king gathered a great force of adherents and forced the rebels to submit. Parliament revoked the charters of enfranchisement, certain leaders were executed without process of law, and the Hathnaughts who had hoped to see all rank and distinctions levelled, were again enslaved.

Thus, while the Black Death emancipated Dennis from serfdom and made him class conscious, the rising of the Hathnaughts under Wat Tyler left him without political liberty, a boon for which he is still battling in our day under Lloyd George and the Labour party.

CHAPTER VII.

DENNIS HATHNAUGHT BECOMES A CITIZEN.

When you say your daily prayers, you should thank Heaven for the mountains and the cities, for they have done much to win you freedom. In Sheridan Knowles' "William Tell" we see how lovingly the Swiss Hathnaught addressed his "crags and peaks," but back of the walls of the cities, no less than in the mountains, embattled Hathnaughts have won charters of liberty in many a hard-fought contest with feudal privileges.

Duruy, in his "Middle Ages," traces the beginning of the communal movement to 1067, when the city of Mens went to war against its overlord. Little by little the burgesses, often with the aid of the kings who wished to break down the vast feudal power, won concession after concession. In "the good old days," a freeman, lingering a year and a day upon the domain of a lord, became, automatically, a serf. In the days when the city began to rise and flourish, the fact that a serf dwelt unchallenged within its walls for a year and a day, made him a freeman. By the twelfth century the serf had become so far acknowledged to be a human being that he

64

could legally give testimony in a court of law.

Guizot (History of Civilization in Europe), discussing the rise of free cities, declares that it was not till the eleventh and twelfth centuries that corporate cities make any figure in history. "I cannot, at this period," he says, "call in the testimony of known and contemporary events, because it was not till between the twelfth and fifteenth centuries that corporations attained any degree of perfection and influence, that those institutions bore any fruit, and that we can verify our assertions by history. . . . But let us enter one of those free cities and see what is going on within it. Here things take quite another turn; we find ourselves in a fortified town, defended by armed burgesses. Those burgesses fix their own taxes, elect their own magistrates, have their own courts of judicature, their own public assemblies for deliberating upon public measures, from which none are excluded. They make war at their own expense, even against their suzerain, maintain their own militia. In short, they govern themselves, they are sovereigns. . . . In the present day the burgesses in a national point of view, are everything—municipalities nothing; formerly corporations were everything, while the burgesses, as respects the nation, were nothing."

Guizot says that from the fifth century to the time of the complete organization of the feudal system, the state of

the times was continually getting worse.
Before that time the towns had retained
some fragments of Roman institutions in
the government of the towns. Upon the
triumph of the feudal system the Hathnaughts of the towns, without falling into
the slavery of the agriculturists, were entirely subjected to the control of a lord,
were included in some fief, and lost, by this
title, somewhat of the independence which
still remained to them.

Guizot continues: "When once, however, the feudal system was fairly established, when every man had taken his
place, and became fixed, as it were, to
the soil; when the wandering life had
entirely ceased, the towns again assumed
some importance—a new activity began
to display itself within them. This is not
surprising. Human activity, as we all
know, is like the fertility of the soil:
when the disturbing process is over, it re-
appears and makes all to glow and blos-
som; wherever there appears the least
glimmering of peace and order the hopes
of man are excited, and with his hopes his
industry. This is what took place in the
cities. No sooner was society a little settled under the feudal system, than the
proprietors of fiefs began to feel new
wants, and to acquire a certain taste for
improvement and melioration; this gave
rise to some little commerce and industry
in the towns of their domains; wealth and
population increased within them—slowly
for certain, but still they increased.

"Among other circumstances which

aided in bringing this about, there is one which, in my·opinion, has not been sufficiently noticed,—I mean the asylum, the protection which the churches afforded to fugitives. Before the free towns were constituted, before they were in a condition by their power, their fortifications, to offer an asylum to the desolate population of the country, when there was no place of safety for them but the church, this circumstance alone was sufficient to draw into the cities many unfortunate persons and fugitives. These sought refuge either in the church itself or within its precincts; it was not merely the lower orders, such as serfs, villeins, and so on, that sought this protection, but frequently men of considerable rank and wealth, who might chance to be proscribed. The chronicles of the times are full of examples of this kind. We find men lately powerful, upon being attacked by some more powerful neighbour, or by the king himself, abandoning their dwellings, and carrying away all the property they could rake together, entering into some city, and placing themselves under the protection of a church: they became citizens. Refugees of this sort had, in my opinion a considerable influence upon the progress of the cities; they introduced into them, besides their wealth, elements of a population superior to the great mass of their inhabitants."

In the old days, men wandered far to pillage, but under the fixed, settled life of the feudal system, the brunt of pillage fell upon the cities.

Guizot says: "The exactions of the proprietors of fiefs upon the burgesses were redoubled at the end of the tenth century. Whenever the lord of the domain, by which a city was girt, felt a desire to increase his wealth, he gratified his avarice at the expense of the citizens.

"It was more particularly at this period that the citizens complained of the total want of commercial security. Merchants on returning from their trading rounds, could not, with safety, return to their city. Every avenue was taken possession of by the lord of the domain and his vassals. The moment in which industry commenced its career was precisely that in which security was most wanting. Nothing is more galling to an active spirit than to be deprived of the long anticipated pleasure of enjoying the fruits of his industry . . . There is in the progressive movement, which elevates a man of a population toward a new fortune, a spirit of resistance against iniquity and violence much more energetic than in any other situation."

It was a time, we read, when there was no settled order, but a perpetual recurrence of individual will, refusing to submit to authority.

"Such," says Guizot, "was the conduct of the major part of the holders of fiefs toward their suzerains, of the small proprietors of land to the greater; so that at the very time when the cities were oppressed and tormented, at the moment when they had new and greater interests to sustain, they had before their eyes a continual lesson of insurrection.

"The feudal system rendered this service to mankind—it has constantly exhibited individual will, displaying itself in all its power and energy— . . . In spite of their weakness, in spite of the prodigious inequality which existed between them and the great proprietors, their lords, the cities everywhere broke out into rebellion against them. . . . Doubtless in the eighth, ninth, and tenth centuries there were many attempts at resistance, many efforts made for freedom:—many attempts to escape from bondage, which not only were unsuccessful, but remained without glory. Still we may rest assured that those attempts had a vast influence upon succeeding events: they kept alive and maintained the spirit of liberty—they prepared the great insurrection of the eleventh century."

Guizot describes the construction of the house of a citizen of the twelfth century so far as one can now obtain an idea of it.

"It consisted usually," he said, "of three stories, one room in each; that on the ground floor served as a general eating-room for the family; the first story was much elevated for the sake of security, and this is the most remarkable circumstance in the construction. The room in this story was the habitation of the master of the house and his wife. The house was, in general, flanked with an angular tower, usually square: another symptom of war; another means of defence. The second story consisted again of a single room; its use is not known, but it probably served for the children and domestics. Above this in most houses, was a small platform, evidently intended as an observatory or watch tower. Every feature of the building bore the appearance of war. This was the decided characteristic, the true name of the movement which wrought out the freedom of the cities. . . . Treaties of peace between the cities and their adversaries were so many charters. These charters of the cities were so many positive treaties of peace between the burgesses and their lords."

These insurrections Guizot regards as spontaneous, growing out of a similarity of oppressions of the Hathnaughts, and in no sense the result of concerted action. Each town rebelled on its own account against its own lord, unconnected with any other place. Royalty, seeking its own advantage sometimes sided with the cities, sometimes with the lords, but altogether, he thinks, produced more of good than of evil. This inevitable interference of royalty, brought on frequent and close connections between the Hathnaughts and the king and the result was the cities became a part of the state and began to have relations with the general government.

Says Guizot: "This formation of a great social class was the necessary result of the local enfranchisement of the burgesses. . . . In the twelfth century, this class was almost entirely composed of merchants or small traders, and little landed or house proprietors who had taken up their residence in the city. Three centuries afterward there were added to this class lawyers, physicians, men of letters, and the local magistrates."

This rise of free citizenship, Guizot points out, resulted in the struggle of classes, "a struggle which constitutes the very fact of modern history, and of which it is full." . . . "No class has been able to overcome, to subject the others; the struggle, instead of rendering society stationary, has been a principal cause of its progress." . . . "The cities themselves, in their turn, entered into the feudal system; they had vassals, and became suzerains; and by this title possessed that portion of sovereignty which was inherent with suzerainty. A great confusion arose between the rights which they held from their feudal position and those which they had acquired by their insurrection; and by this double title they held the sovereignty.

"Let us see, as far as the very scanty sources left us will allow, how the internal government of the cities, at least in the more early times, was managed. The entire body of the inhabitants formed the communal assembly; all those who had taken the communal oath—and all who dwelt within the walls were obliged to do so—were summoned, by the tolling of the bell, to the general assembly. In this was named the magistrates. The number chosen, and the power and proceedings of the magistrates, differed very considerably. After choosing the magistrates, the assemblies dissolved; and the magistrates governed almost alone, sufficiently arbitrarily, being under no further responsibility than the new elections, or perhaps, popular outbreaks which were, at this time, the great guarantee for good government. . . . It was impossible, especially while such manners prevailed, to establish anything like a regular government with proper guarantees of order and duration. The greater part of the population of these cities were ignorant, brutal and savage to a degree which rendered them exceedingly difficult to govern."

Inevitably, as Guizot shows, there was formed a burgess aristocracy, and a system of privileges was introduced into the cities, resulting in great inequality. There grew up in all the cities, a number of opulent burgesses and a population more or less numerous of Hathnaughts who, despite their inferiority, were not without influence. The superior citizens, he says, found themselves pressed between two great difficulties: first, the arduous one of governing the turbulent Hathnaughts; and secondly, that of withstanding the continual attempts of the ancient master of the borough, who sought to regain his former power. Such, he says, was the situation of their affairs, not only in France, but in Europe down to the sixteenth century.

Wolfgang Menzel (History of Germany) declares that the cities of the Teutonic races, insignificant in origin, gradually rose to a height of power that made it possible for them to defy the authority of the sovereign and to become the most powerful support of the empire. Particularly interesting to the student of industrialism is his description of the German Guilds. You will note all through his account, that Fritz Hathnaught is entitled to wear service stripes as a Soldier in the army of human liberty. Listen to Menzel:

"Increasing civilization had produced numerous wants, which commerce and industry alone supply. The people, moreover, oppressed by the feudal system in the country, sheltered themselves beneath the ægis of the city corporations. The artisans, although originally serfs, were always free. In many cities the air bestowed freedom; whoever dwelt within their walls could not be reduced to a state of vassalage, and was instantly affranchised, although formerly a serf when dwelling beyond the wall.

"In the thirteenth century, every town throughout Flanders enjoyed this privilege. It was only in the villages that fell, at a later period, under the jurisdiction of the towns, that the peasants still remained in a state of vassalage. The emperors, who beheld in the independence and power of the cities, a defense against the princes and popes, readily bestowed great privileges upon them, and released them from the jurisdiction of the lords of the country, the bishops, and the imperial governors. The cities often asserted their own independence, the power of a bishop being unable to cope with that of a numerous and high-spirited body of citizens. They also increased their extent at the expense of the provincial nobility, by throwing down their castles, by taking their serfs as Pfahlburger (suburbans) or by purchasing their lands.

"The imperial free cities had the right of prescribing their own laws which were merely ratified by the emperor. . . . To the right of legislation was added that of independent jurisdiction, which was denoted by the pillars known as Roland's pillars, and by the red towers. The red flag was the sign of penal judicature, and red towers were used as prisons for criminals; and as the practice of torture became more general in criminal cases, torture, famine, witch and heretic towers were erected in almost every town. The management of the town affairs was at length entirely entrusted to the council, which originally consisted of the sheriffs headed by a mayor, but was afterward chiefly composed of members elected from the different parishes, and was at length compelled to admit among its number the presidents of the various guilds; and the mayor, the president of the ancient burgesses, was, consequently, replaced by the burgomaster, or president of the guilds. The right of self-government was denoted by the bell on the town or council house, in the Middle Ages the greatest pride of the provincial cities, which had gained independence. . . . The guilds ere long grasped at greater privileges, and formed a democratic party which aimed at wresting the management of the town business out of the hands of the aristocratic burghers.

"The corporations corresponded with the ancient German Guilds. The artisan entered as an apprentice, became partner, and finally master. The apprentice, like the knightly squire, was obliged to travel. The completion of a masterpiece was required before he could become a master. Illegitimate birth and immorality excluded the artisan from the guild. Each guild was strictly superintended by a tribune. Every member of a guild was assisted when in need by the society. Every disagreement between the members was put a stop to, as injurious to the whole body. The members of one corporation generally dwelt in one particular street, had their common station in the market, their distinguishing colors, and a part assigned to them in guarding the city, etc. These guilds chiefly conduced to bring art and handicraft to perfection."

The rise of the English town is described by Green. "If," he says, "we pass from the English university to the English town, we see a progress as important and hardly less interesting. In their origin our boroughs were utterly unlike those of the rest of the ancient world. The cities of Italy and Provence had preserved the municipal institutions of their

Roman past; the German towns had been
founded by Henry the Fowler with the
purpose of sheltering industry from the
feudal oppression around them; the communes of Northern France sprang into
existence in revolt against feudal outrage within their wall.

"But in England the traditions of Rome
passed utterly away, while feudal oppression was held fairly in check by the
Crown. The English town therefore was
in its beginning simply a piece of the general country, organized and governed precisely in the same manner as the townships around it. Its existence witnessed
indeed to the need which was felt in those
earlier times of mutual help and protection. The burgh or borough was probably
a more defensible place than the common
village; it may have had a ditch or mound
about it instead of the quickset hedge or
tun from which the town took its name.
But in itself it was simply a township or
group of townships where men clustered,
whether for trade or defense more thickly
than elsewhere. . . ."

"Towns like Bristol were the direct result of trade. There was the same variety in the mode in which the various
town communities were formed. While
the bulk of them grew by simple increase
of population from township to town,
larger boroughs, such as York with its
six shires, or London with its wards and
sokes and franchises, show how families
and groups of settlers settled down side
by side, and claimed as they coalesced,

each for itself, its shire or share of the town-ground, while jealously preserving its individual life within the town community. But strange as these aggregations might be, the constitution of the borough which resulted from them was simply that of the people at large. Whether we regard it as a township, or rather from its size as a hundred or collection of townships, the obligations of the dwellers within its bounds were those of the townships round, to keep fence and trench in good repair, to send a contingent to the fyrd and a reeve and four men to the hundred court and shire court.

"As in other townships, land was a necessary accompaniment of freedom. The landless man who dwelt in a borough had no share in its corporate life: for purposes of government or property the town consisted simply of the landed proprietors within its bounds.

"The common lands which are still attached to many of the boroughs take us back to a time when each township lay within a ring or mark of open ground which served at once as boundary and pasture land. Each of the four wards of York had its common pasture; Oxford has still its own 'Portmeadow.'

"The inner life of the borough lay as in the township about it, in the hands of its own freemen, gathered in borough-moot or portmannimote. But the social change brought about by the Danish wars, the legal requirement that each man should have a lord, affected the towns as it affected the rest of the country. Some passed into the hands of great thanes near to them; the bulk became known as in the demesne of the king. A new officer, the lord's or king's reeve, was a sign of this revolution. It was the reeve who first summoned the borough-moot and administered justice in it; it was he who collected the lord's dues or annual rent of the town, and who exacted the services it owed to its lord.

"To modern eyes these services would imply almost complete subjection. When Leicester, for instance, passed from the hands of the Conqueror into those of its earls, its townsmen were bound to reap their lord's corn-crops, to grind at his mill, to redeem their strayed cattle from his pound. The great forest around was the earl's, and it was only out of his grace that the little borough could drive its swine into the woods or pasture its cattle in the glades. The justice and the government of a town lay wholly in its master's hands; he appointed its bailiffs, received the fines and forfeitures of his tenants, and the fees and tolls of their markets and fairs."

"But," continues Green rather naïvely in view of the fact that the Englishman has been stripped of all save his trousers, "when once these dues were paid and these services rendered, the English townsman was practically free. His rights were as rigidly defined by custom as those of his lord. Property and person alike were secured against arbitrary seizure. He could demand a fair trial on any charge, and even if justice was administered by his master's reeve, it was administered in the presence and with the assent of his fellow townsmen.

"The bell which swung out from the town tower gathered the burgesses to a common meeting, where they could exercise rights of free speech and free deliberation on their own affairs. Their merchant guild, over its ale-feast, regulated trade, distributed the sums due from the towns among the different burgesses, looked to the due repairs of gate and wall, and acted, in fact, pretty much the same as the town council of to-day. . . . In the quiet quaintly named streets and town mead and market place, in the lord's mill beside the stream, in the bell that swung out its summons to the crowded boroughmote, in merchant-guild, and church-guild and craft-guild, lay the life of Englishmen who were doing more than knight and baron to make England what she is, the life of their homes and their trade, of their sturdy battle with oppression, their steady ceaseless struggle for right and freedom.

"London stood first among English towns and the privileges which its citizens won became precedents for the burghers of meaner boroughs. Even at the conquest its power and wealth secured it a full recognition of all its ancient privileges from the Conqueror. In one way indeed it profited by the revolution which laid England at the feet of the stranger. One immediate result of William's success was an immigration into England from the Continent. A peaceful invasion of the Norman traders followed quick on the invasion of the Norman soldiery. Every Norman noble as he quartered himself upon English lands, every Norman abbot as he entered his English cloister, gathered French artists, French shopkeepers, French domestics about him."

But Dennis Hathnaught is coming into his own, and in our day, centuries of struggle against oppression are crystallizing into ideas of municipal regulation and government that make English cities important in the study of economic development. More than any other class in Britain, Dennis Hathnaught is entitled to the honour of posing for a statue of John Bull. John's square jaw is the evolution of the first grim resolution of the Hathnaughts to give tyranny the hurry call to the exit.

CHAPTER VIII.

DENNIS FOUNDS THE HANSEATIC LEAGUE.

It may sound paradoxical to credit Dennis Hathnaught with the founding of such a powerful and opulent organization as the Hanseatic League, but when one understands that the great bourgeois class of the Middle Ages—as indeed of all ages—was recruited from the lower order of society it is but historic justice to add the Hanseatic League to the roll of Hathnaught's achievements.

The Lords of Have-and-Hold, being essentially a robber class, founded on conquest, thievery, and the mailed fist, would never think of such an orderly thing as the organization of trade and the accumulating of wealth through the medium of honest barter. Indeed, the entire history of the League is filled with incidents of titled freebooters and their mobs of retainers swooping down upon the traders and enriching themselves through tribute and pillage.

The Hanseatic League was first an organization of German merchants, and this developed into a commercial union of certain German towns. Its rise is generally understood to date from 1241, when Lubeck and Hamburg formed an alliance. It had factories or trading stations in Wisby, London, Novgorod, Bergen, and Bruges. The aims of the League were mainly to improve conditions for their merchants abroad and establish a greater unity among the towns with a view to improving trade efficiency. In England the merchants were called Easterlings, whence the present word sterling.

Thanks to the efforts of the Historical Society of the Hanseatic Cities, we are destined to possess a fruitful literature on this interesting subject. There are two able works in German on the Hanseatic League. One by Georg Sartorius (Geschichte des hanseatischen Bundes) traces the growth and ultimate decadence of the League in a way that makes the work still authoritative, even though fuller material than the author worked with is now available. E. Dietrich Schafer in his work on the subject had an advantage over Sartorius, for the researches of the Historical Society of the Hanseatic Cities were accessible to him. So that while he does not altogether supplant Sartorius, his work is held to be a greater authority.

Wolfgang Menzel, in his "History of Germany," devotes considerable space to the League. His work is available for English readers in a translation by Mrs. George Horrocks.

"The power of the princes in Germany," he says, "was counterpoised by that of the cities, which, sensible of their inability individually to assert their liberty, endangered by the absence and subsequent ruin of the Emperor, had mutually entered into an offensive and defensive alliance. The cities on the Northern Ocean and the Baltic vied with those of Lombardy in denseness of population, and in the assertion of their independence. Their fleet returned from the East laden with glory. They conquered Lisbon, besieged Accon and Damietta, founded the order of German Hospitalers, and gained great part of Livonia and Prussia. A strict union existed among their numerous merchants. Every city possessed a corporation or guild, consisting, according to the custom of the times, of masters, partners, and apprentices. These guilds were armed and formed the chief strength of the city.

"Ghent and Bruges were the first cities in Flanders which became noted for their civil privileges, their manufactories, commerce, and industry. In the twelfth century they had already formed a Hansa, a great commercial association in which seventeen cities took part. In the thirteenth century, their example was followed by the commercial towns on the Rhine, the Elbe, and the Baltic, but on a larger scale, the new Hansa, forming a political as well as a commercial association, which was commenced by Lubeck, between which and Hamburg a treaty was made, A. D. 1241, in which Bremen and almost every city in the north of Germany as far as Cologne and Brunswick joined."

Something of their power is shown by

Menzel in the stories he tells of the Lübeck fleet worsting Erich IV of Denmark, and the citizens of Bremen pulling down a custom house the archbishop had erected, and asserting their independence A. D. 1246. . . .

Flanders, he says, far surpassed other countries in her municipal privileges, art, and industry, possessed the first great commercial navy, and founded the first great commercial league or Hansa in the twelfth century.

"This example," he continues, "the first subjection of the Wends on the Baltic, and the crusades, greatly increased the activity of commerce in the thirteenth century on the Rhine, the Elbe, and the Baltic. The crusades were undertaken in a mercantile as well as a religious point of view. In the East the merchant pilgrims formed themselves into the German order of knighthood, and, on their return to their native country, leagued together, A. D. 1241, for the purpose of defending th its against the native princes, and their commerce against the attack of the foreigner.

"This Hansa League extended to such a degree in the thirteenth and fourteenth centuries as sometimes to include upward of seventy cities; its fleets ruled the Northern Ocean, conquered entire countries, and reduced powerful sovereigns to submission. The union that existed between the cities was, nevertheless, far from firmly cemented, and the whole of its immense force, was, from want of unanimity, seldom brought to bear at once upon its enemies. A single attempt would have placed the whole of Northern Germany within its power, had the policy of the citizens been other than mercantile, and had they not been merely intent upon forcing the temporal and spiritual lords to trade with them upon the most favourable conditions."

Lübeck, Menzel says, was the metropolis of the whole league, where the directory of the Hansa, the general archive and treasury were kept, and where the great Hansa diets were held by the deputies from all the Hanse towns, in which they took into deliberation commercial speculations, the arming of fleets, peace, and war.

Menzel continues, "At Bruges, the Hansa merely possessed a depot for their goods, which passed hence into the hands of the Italians. The Colognese merchants possessed a second great depot as early as 1203, in London, still known as Guildhall, the hall of the merchants' guild of Cologne. At a later period, the Hansa monopolized the whole commerce of England. At Bergen, in Norway, the Hansa possessed a third and extremely remarkable colony, 3,000 Hanseatic merchants, masters, and apprentices living there like monks without any women. The Hanseatic colonists were generally forbidden to marry lest they should take possession of the country in which they lived and deprive the League of it. The fourth great depot was founded at Novgorod, in

the north of Russia, A. D. 1277. By it
the ancient commercial relations between
the coasts of the Baltic and Asia were
preserved and the Hansa traded by land
with Asia at first through Riga, but on
the expulsion of the Tartars from Russia
and the subjection of Novgorod by the
Tzars, through Breslau, Erfurt, Magde-
burg, and Leipzig. Germany and Europe
were thus supplied with spices, silks,
jewels, etc., from Asia; with furs, iron,
and immense quantities of herrings from
the North. France principally traded in
salt, while Germany exported beer and
wine, corn, linen, and arms; Bohemia,
metals and precious stones; and Flanders,
fine linen and cloths of every description.

"The ferocity of the Hungarians, Ser-
vians, and Wallachians, and the enmity
of the Greeks, effectually closed the Dan-
ube, the natural outlet for the produce of
the interior of Germany toward Asia. The
traffic on this stream during the Crusades
raised Ulm, and, at a later period, Augs-
berg, to considerable importance.

"The traffic on the Rhine was far more
considerable, notwithstanding the heavy
customs levied by the barbarous princes
and knights which the Rhinish league
was annually compelled to oppose and put
down by force.

"Cologne was the grand depot for the
whole of the inland commerce. Goods
were brought here from every quarter of
the globe, and, according to a Hanseatic
law, no merchant coming from the West,
from Flanders or Spain, was allowed to

pass with his goods further than Cologne; none coming from the East, not even the Dutch, could mount, and none from the upper country descend, the Rhine beyond that city. The highroads were naturally in a bad state, and infested with toll-gatherers and robbers. The merchants were compelled to purchase a safe-conduct along the worst roads, or to clear them by force of arms. Most of the roads were laid by the merchants with the permission of well-disposed princes. Thus, for instance, the rich burgher, Henry Cunter of Botzen, laid the road across the rocks until then impassable, on the Eisack, between Botzen and Brixen, A. D. 1304; travellers up to that period, having been compelled to make a wearisome detour through Meran and Jauffen.

"The lace and cloth manufactures of the Flemish, which lent increased splendour to the courts, the wealthy, and the high-born, were the first that rose into note, the Hansa being merely occupied with trade and commercial monopoly. Ulm afterward attempted to compete with the Italian manufacturers; but Nuremberg, on account of her central position, less attracted by foreign commerce, became the first town of manufacturing repute in Germany.

"The trade with the rich East, and the silver mines discovered in the tenth century in the Harz, in the twelfth, in the Erz Mountains in Bohemia, brought more money into circulation. The ancient Hohlpfennigs (solidi, shillings), of which there were twenty-two to a pound (and twelve denarii to a shilling) were replaced by the heavy Groschen (solidi grossi), of which there were sixty to a silver mark, and by the albus or white pennies, which varied in value. The working of the Bohemian mines in the fourteenth century, brought the broad Prague Groschen into note; they were reckoned by scores, always by sixties, the cardinal number in Bohemia. The smaller copper coins, or Heller (from hohl, hollow; halb, half; or from the free imperial town, Halle) were weighed by the pound, the value of which was two gulden, which at a later period, when silver became more common, rose to three."

But the League went the way of earth at last. Its last days are well described by Edgar Sanderson: (History of the World) "The decline of this great trade-confederation began with a change in the movement of the herring. Early in the fifteenth century the fish deserted the Baltic spawning grounds for the German Ocean; the Netherlands gained what the Hansa towns of the eastern sea had lost; and Amsterdam, in a large degree, took the place of Lübeck, which, in the fourteenth century had a population approaching the double of its numbers in 1870. The wealth, pride, and power of these northern commercial towns waned further after the change of commercial routes due to the discovery of America and of the way to India around the Cape.

The Dutch members of the Confederacy had left it early in the fifteenth century, and the rise of British commerce in Tudor days had its influence, while the Reformation, changing the religion of northern Europe, lessened the demand for wax for candles as well as for the salt fish in which some of the towns still traded. Early in the seventeenth century Lubeck, Hamburg, and Bremen were the only survivors of the League, and these three famous free cities, after the middle of the nineteenth century relinquished their old privileges as free ports by incorporation into the German Zoll Verein, or Customs Union."

Sanderson pays a tribute to the noble part played by the League in "spreading civilization through regions of Europe sunk in barbarism, and by maintaining the cause of right against might."

Had the League been less intent upon trade it might have founded a great and powerful industrial empire, but its members, so long as trade was unhampered, did not interfere with the ambitions of princes and had no wish to govern. We should like to see it still flourishing under the motto "Esto perpetua," but as this was not to be, let us inscribe upon its tomb, "Requiescat in pace."

CHAPTER IX.

FRITZ HATHNAUGHT AND THE PEASANTS' WAR.

One of the greatest struggles of a despised, oppressed and exploited people to drop the burden from the back and assume the erect stature of freemen, was that of Fritz Hathnaught in sixteenth century Germany. This "Peasants' War" as it is known in history, started in 1524, spread rapidly, and was not suppressed until 1525.

"The religious liberty preached by Luther," says Menzel (History of Germany), "was understood by them as also implying the political freedom for which they sighed. Their condition had greatly deteriorated during the past century. The nobility had bestowed the chief part of their wealth on the church and dissipated the remainder at court. Luxury had also greatly increased, and the peasant was consequently laden with feudal dues of every description, to which were added their ill-treatment by the men-at-arms and mercenaries maintained at their expense, the damage done by game, the destruction of the crops by the noble followers of the chase, and finally, the extortions practiced by the new law-offices, the wearisome written proceedings, and the impoverishment consequent on lawsuits. The German peasant, despised and enslaved, could no longer seek refuge from the tyranny of his liege in the cities, where the reception of fresh suburbans was strictly prohibited, and where the citizen, enervated by wealth and luxury, instead of siding with the peasant, imitated the noble and viewed him with contempt."

Menzel enumerates the twelve articles that the Hathnaughts wished to submit to a court of arbitration, as follows: "First —the right of the peasantry to appoint their own preachers who were to be allowed to preach the word of God from the Bible. Second—That the dues paid by the peasantry were to be abolished with the exception of tithes ordained by God for the maintenance of the clergy, the surplus of which was to be applied to general purposes and to the maintenance of the poor. Third—The abolition of vassalage as iniquitous. Fourth—The right of hunting, fishing and fowling. Fifth— That of cutting wood in the forests. Sixth—The modification of socage and average service. Seventh—That the peasant should be guaranteed from the caprice of his lord by a fixed agreement. Eighth—The modification of the rent upon feudal lands, by which a part of the profit would be secured to the occupant. Ninth—The administration of justice according to the ancient laws, not according to the new statutes and to caprice. Tenth—The restoration of communal property, illegally seized. Eleventh—The abolition of dues on the death of a serf, by which the widow and orphans were deprived of their right. Twelfth—The acceptance of the aforesaid articles or their refutation as contrary to Scripture."

Although they had named Luther as a possible member of a court of arbitration, he refused to interfere in their affairs, dreading, according to Menzel, the insolence of the Hathnaughts under the guidance of Anabaptists and enthusiasts. He used his utmost efforts to put down the insurrection, and was accused by Thomas Munzer, one of the Hathnaughts, of "deserting the cause of liberty and of rendering the Reformation a fresh advantage for the princes, a fresh means of tyranny."

For a time the Hathnaughts had for a leader, Goetz von Berlichingen, a notorious robber, who forms the subject of a drama by Goethe, who idealizes the bandit and his character. Menzel describes him as an ordinary highwayman. He had lost a hand by a cannon shot and in its place had an iron hand.

When the revolt was put down, "The city of Wurzburg," according to Menzel, "threw open her gates to the triumphant Truchsess who held a fearful court of judgment in which the prisoners were beheaded by his jester, Hans." In a note to the text, Menzel adds: "The

peasants knelt in a row before the Truchsess, while Hans the Jester, with the
sword of execution in his hand, marched
up and down behind them. The Truchsess demanded; 'which among them had
been implicated in the revolt?' None
acknowledged the crime. 'Which of
them had read the Bible?' Some said
yes, some no, and each of those who replied in the affirmative was instantly deprived of his head by Hans, amid the
loud laughter of the squires. The same
fate befell those who knew how to read
or write. The priest of Schipf, an old,
gouty man, who had zealously opposed
the peasantry, had himself carried by
four of his men to the Truchsess in order
to receive the thanks of that prince for
his services; but Hans, imagining that
he was one of the rebels, suddenly step-
ping behind him, cut off his head. Upon
which, the Truchsess relates, 'I seriously
reproved my good Hans for his untoward
jest.' "

These butchers were fit ancestors of
the despoilers of Belgium. Menzel declares that in this slaughter of the Hathnaughts, which was general, the spiritual
princes surpassed their lay brethren in
atrocity. In a later revolt of a more religious nature under Thomas Munzer,
which broke out in Thuringia in the
summer of 1525, the peasants were de-
feated at Frankenhausen with great
slaughter, and Munzer, found secreted
in a haystack, was put to the rack and
executed. In all, more than one hun-

dred thousand of the Hathnaughts fell in this terrible struggle, and at the end the survivors were worse off than ever.

According to Menzel the misery of the Hathnaughts was by no means so great during the Middle Ages as it became after the great peasant war of 1525. All through the ages will ring the wail of the poor peasant boy, victim of oppression and malnutrition, who did not fear death so much as he regretted the fact that he never had enjoyed a good dinner: "Alas! Alas! must I die so soon, and I have scarcely had a bellyful twice in my life!"

CHAPTER X.

DENNIS IN SIXTEENTH CENTURY ENGLAND.

From the Norman Conquest to the accession of Henry VIII, a period of five centuries, Saxon and Norman were gradually disappearing, and out of the great melting pot of the nation there came the modern Englishman. We have seen how oppressive was the government of the Conqueror, yet this very oppression which aimed at the centralization of authority in the king, brought the barons in self-defence into alliance with the burghers.

"Thus," says Duruy, in chorus with Buckle and Bonnemere, "the nobles saved their rights only by securing those of their humblest allies. In this manner of agreement between the burgher middle class and the nobles, English public liberty was founded."

The Normans seemed more bent upon robbing the people through unjust taxation than in building up a strong government with a united people, speaking a common language and with a common destiny. But insensibly the Norman and Saxon elements were fusing; the union was hastened by the wresting of the Magna Charta from King John in 1215, and the poems of Chaucer, and Wyclif's translation of the Bible, blended the current speech of both races into that glorious tongue that finally burst into full splendour in the age of Elizabeth.

When Henry VIII ascended the throne he reigned over a genuine English people. Old animosities had disappeared, and there were few in the nation that could tell on which side their ancestors had fought at Hastings.

James Anthony Froude in the first chapter of his "History of England," has an interesting survey of the social condition of the Hathnaughts in sixteenth century England. He treats in turn of mediæval civilization; the encouragement of manufactures; the decline of the towns; the feudal system; the distribution of property; wages and prices; labour and capital; management of land; the commercial spirit; absorption of land for pasturage; income of the higher classes; clergy and laity; education; organization of trade; the London Companies; handloom weavers.

In the time of Henry VIII there was passed a statute for the encouragement of the linen trade and thus to bring about the better employment of the people. "This act," says Froude, "was designed immediately to keep wives and children of the poor in work in their own houses; but it leaves no doubt that manufactures in England had not of themselves that tendency to self-development which would encourage an enlarging population. The woolen manufactures similarly appear, from the many statutes upon them, to have been **vigorous** at a fixed level, but to have shown no tendency to rise beyond that level. With a fixed market and a fixed demand production continued uniform."

Froude notes the general decay of the towns in 1540 during Henry VIII's reign and a decline of manufactures despite statutory encouragement. But he explains this by saying that the old towns were built, not for industry, but for the protection of property and life, and as the country had become secure, one of the purposes of the towns was no longer required. The woolen manufacture in Worcestershire, he says, was spreading into the open country and doubtless into other counties, too.

"It was in fact," observes Froude, "the first symptom of the impending revolution." . . . "This mighty change, however, was long in silent progress before it began to tell on the institutions of the country. When city burghers bought estates, the law insisted jealously on their accepting with them all the feudal obligations. Attempts to use the land as a 'commodity' were angrily repressed; while again, such persons endeavoured, as they do at present, to cover the recent origin of their families by adopting the manners of the nobles instead of transferring the habits of the towns to the parks and chases of the English counties. The old English organization maintained its full activity; and the duties of property continued to be for another century more considered than its rights."

Villanage in the reign of Henry VIII had practically ceased, but Froude shows that Hathnaught was far from being his own master; nor might he be idle or leave his employment at will or through caprice.

"Through all these arrangements," says Froude, "a single aim is visible; that every man in England should have his definite place and definite duty assigned to him, and that no human being should be at liberty to lead at his own pleasure an unaccountable existence." He goes on to discuss the respective advantages of large and small estates— peasant proprietary or a constantly diminishing number of wealthy landlords, but takes no sides himself.

"Dress," he continues, "which now scarcely suffices to distinguish the master from his servant, was then the symbol of rank, prescribed by statute to the various orders of society as strictly as the regimental uniform to officers and privates; diet was also prescribed and with equal strictness." What was eaten and the amount that might be partaken of, was duly set forth in the law. There was nothing in those days that might be likened to the so-called "lobster palaces" of Broadway, New York.

"The state of the working classes," says Froude, "can, however, be more certainly determined by a comparison of their wages with the prices of food. Both

were regulated, as far as regulation was
possible, by act of parliament, and we
have therefore data of the clearest kind
by which to judge. The majority of
agricultural labourers lived in the houses
of their employers; this, however, was
not the case with all, and if we can
satisfy ourselves as to the rate at which
those among the poor were able to live
who had cottages of their own, we may
be assured that the rest did not live
worse at their master's tables."

Ye who rail against the high cost of
living, give heed to these prices fixed
by law and quoted by Froude: "Beef
and pork were a half penny a pound,
mutton was three farthings. These were
fixed at these prices by the 3d of the
24th of Henry VIII." . . . "The best
pig or goose in a country market could
be bought for fourpence; a good capon
for threepence or fourpence; a chicken
for a penny; a hen for twopence." Froude
estimates that a penny in terms of Hathnaught's necessities must have been nearly equal in the reign of Henry VIII to
the present shilling.

"Turning then to the table of wages,"
he says, "it will be easy to ascertain his
position. By the 3d of the 6th of Henry
VIII it was enacted that master car-
penters, masons, bricklayers, tylers,
plumbers, glaziers, joiners, and other employers of such skilled workmen, should
give to each of their journeymen, if
no meat or drink was allowed, sixpence
a day for the half year, five pence a

day for the other half; or five pence-half penny for the yearly average. The common labourers were to receive four pence a day for half the year, for the remaining half, three pence. In the harvest months they were allowed to work by the piece, and might earn considerably more."

Commenting upon this in a foot-note and citing authorities, Froude says: "The wages were fixed at a maximum, showing that labour was scarce, and that its natural tendency was toward a higher rate of remuneration. Persons not possessed of other means of subsistence were punishable if they refused to work at the statutable rate of payment; and a clause in the act of Henry VIII directed that where the practice had been to give lower wages, lower wages should be taken. This provision was owing to a difference in the value of money in different parts of England. The price of bread at Stratford, for instance, was permanently twenty-five per cent. below the price in London." . . . "In 1581 the Agricultural labourer as he now exists was only beginning to appear." . . . "This novel class had been called into being by the general raising of rents, and the wholesale eviction of the smaller tenantry which followed the Reformation."

Harrison in his "Description of England," quoted by Froude, says he knew old men, who, comparing things present with things past, spoke of two things grown to be very grievous—to wit, the enhancing of rents and the daily oppression of copyholders, whose lords seek to bring their poor tenants almost into plain servitude and misery, daily devising new means, and seeking up all the old, how to cut them shorter and shorter; doubling, trebling, and now and then seven times increasing their fines; driving them also for every trifle to lose and forfeit their tenures, by whom the greatest part of the realm doth stand and is maintained, to the end they may fleece them yet more; which is a lamentable hearing."

For all his supposed advantage the labourer was not contented. "The wages act of Henry VIII," says Froude, "was unpopular with the labourers, and was held to deprive them of an opportunity of making better terms for themselves." . . . "On the one side parliament interfered to protect employers against their labourers; but it was equally determined that employers should not be allowed to abuse their opportunities; and this directly appears from the 4th of the 5th of Elizabeth, by which, on the most trifling appearance of a depreciation in the currency, it was declared that the labouring man could no longer live on the wages assigned to him by the act of Henry; and a sliding scale was instituted by which, for the future, wages should be adjusted to the price of food."

This method of trying to adjust prices to the purchasing power we find, in "The

Common People of Ancient Rome," by
Professor Frank S. Abbott, was worked
out in the days of Diocletian 301 A. D.
It was not a success, for imperial and
kingly edicts cannot supplant the natural
laws of political economy. Professor Abbott, following the line of Froude, shows
the prices of different articles of food
in the days of Diocletian and the wages
paid the free labourers.

Froude, writing of the towns, the trading and manufacturing classes, says:
"The names and shadows linger about
London of certain ancient societies, the
members of which may still occasionally
be seen in quaint gilt barges pursuing
their own difficult way among the swarm-
ing steamers; while on certain days, the
traditions concerning which are fast dying out of memory, the Fishmongers'
Company, the Goldsmiths' Company, the
Mercers' Company make procession down
the river for civic feasting at Greenwich
or Blackwall. The stately tokens of
ancient honour still belong to them, and
the remnants of ancient wealth and patronage and power. Their charters may
be read by curious antiquaries, and the
bills of fare of their ancient entertainment. But for what purpose they were
called into being, what there was in those
associations of common trades to sur-
round with gilded insignia, and how they
came to be possessed of broad lands and
church preferments, few people now care
to think or inquire. Trade and traders
have no dignity any more in the eyes

of anyone, except what money lends to them; and these outward symbols scarcely rouse even a passing feeling of curiosity. And yet these companies were once something more than mere names. They are all which now remain of a vast organization which once penetrated the entire trading life of England—an organization set on foot to realize that most necessary, if most difficult, condition of commercial excellence under which man shall deal faithfully with his brother, and all wares offered for sale of whatever kind, should honestly be what they are pretended to be."

Under the Guild system, according to Froude, no one was permitted to supply articles which he had not been educated to manufacture; the price at which articles ought justly to be sold was determined; and care was taken to see that cloth put up for sale was true cloth, of true texture and full weight; and so on through the list with all other goods, in the effort to enforce honest dealing.

In London a central council sat for every branch of trade and this council acted in conjunction with the chancellor and the crown. The council fixed prices, wages, arranged rules of apprenticeship. There were searchers who, in company with the Lord Mayor, or other official, inspected the shops of traders. When necessary, suggestions in reports submitted to the state authorities by the guilds, not infrequently became law through statute enactment.

It was the age of the apprentice. No one might open a trade or become a manufacturer unless he had served his full apprenticeship.

There was some notion of the vocational idea in those days, for no man, according to Froude, might work at a business for which he was unfit, and the state insisted on its natural right that children should not be allowed to grow up in idleness, to be returned at mature age upon its hands.

Says Froude: "The children of those who could afford the small entrance fees were apprenticed to trades, the rest were apprenticed to agriculture; and if children were found growing up idle, and their fathers or their friends failed to prove that they were able to secure them an ultimate maintenance, the mayors in towns and the magistrates in the country had authority to take possession of such children, and apprentice them as they saw fit, that when they grew up they might not be driven by want or incapacity to dishonest courses."

Froude observes that it would be madness to try to apply to the changed condition of the present those trade regulations of the Plantagenets and the Tudors, but he suggests that it would be well if some competent person made these laws the subject of a special treatise. Under this iron discipline trade was regulated by law, some of the laws being salutary, but others vexatious, as in the "act touching weavers," which, limiting weavers living in towns to two looms, tended to prevent the cloth manufacture from falling into the power of large capitalists employing hands.

We complain of the short weight grocer and the impure food vender, but there were such in the days of the much married Henry VIII. We read in Froude of complaints made by the leather trade of searchers who, for a bribe, affixed their seal to goods imperfectly tanned, to the great deceit of the buyers thereof." Excessive fees were often imposed, too, upon apprentices in defiance of the law. The custom of skinning your tribe is an old one, Dennis.

Toulmin Smith, in his "English Guilds," traces the original ordinances of more than a hundred early English Guilds. Lujo Brentano in a preliminary essay narrates the history and development of the guilds. This work is held to be the standard authority on the subject. Brentano deals with the origin of guilds; religious and social guilds; town guilds or merchant guilds; craft guilds and tradesunions. Craft guilds are usually held to have been the beginnings of the tradesunions, but they differed from the modern union in that the membership included masters. Thus the guild might act in times of trouble as a board of arbitration and conciliation. The guild was really labour's first great progressive stand against the continuance of the feudal system as shown in a previous chapter.

CHAPTER XI.

DENNIS IN SEVENTEENTH CENTURY ENGLAND.

Macaulay's History of England shall be our authority, for the industrial history of Merrie England in the Seventeenth Century. His brilliant work contains but a few pages concerning the actual life of the Hathnaughts, but this is because of the scantiness of the materials.

"The most numerous class," he says, "is precisely the class respecting which we have the most meager information. In those times philanthropists did not yet regard it as a sacred duty, nor had demagogues yet found it a lucrative trade to talk and write about the distress of the labourer. History was too much occupied with courts and camps to spare a line for the hut of the peasant or the garret of the mechanic. The press now often sends forth in a day a greater quantity of discussion and declamation about the condition of the working man than was published during the twenty-eight years which elapsed between the Restoration and the Revolution. . . .

"The great criterion of the state of

the common people is the amount of
their wages; and as four-fifths of the
common people were, in the seventeenth
century, employed in agriculture, it is
especially important to ascertain what
were the wages of agricultural industry.
. . . Sir William Petty (Political Arith-
metic), whose mere assertion carries
great weight, informs us that a labourer
was by no means in the lowest state who
received for a day's work four-pence
with food or eight-pence without food.
Four shillings a week therefore were,
according to Petty's calculation, fair agricultural wages. . . .

"About the beginning of the year 1685
the justices of Warwickshire, in the
exercise of a power entrusted to them
by an Act of Elizabeth, fixed, at their
quarter sessions, a scale of wages for
the county, and notified that every employer who gave more than the author-
ized sum, and every working man who
received more, would be liable to punishment."

In some places the Hathnaughts were
more favoured, and Macaulay cites Richard Dunning, a gentleman of Devonshire,
as authority for the statement that the
wages of the Devonshire Dennis were, in
1685, without food, five shillings a week.
In the neighbourhood of Bury Saint Ed-
munds, Macaulay asserts, conditions were
even better, for the magistrates of Suf-
folk in the spring of 1682 decreed that
where a Hathnaught was not boarded he
should have five shillings a week in

winter and six in summer. In 1661 the justices of Chelmsford fixed the wages of Essex Hathnaughts who were not boarded, at six shillings in winter and seven in summer.

Macaulay points out that in the years in which this order was made, necessaries of life were immoderately dear. "Wheat was at seventy shillings the quarter, which would even now be considered as almost a famine price." . . .

The average wage of his own day, Macaulay observes, was very much higher, and in prosperous counties the weekly wages of Hathnaughts engaged in farm work amounted to twelve, fourteen, and even sixteen shillings. He continues: "The remuneration of workmen employed in manufactures has always been higher than that of tillers of the soil. In the year 1680, a member of the House of Commons remarked that the high wages paid in this country made it impossible for our textures to maintain a competition with the produce of the Indian looms. An English mechanic, he said, instead of slaving like a native of Bengal for a piece of copper, exacted a shilling a day."

Because of the inattention formerly paid to the Hathnaughts, a great deal of their history, Macaulay says, may be learned only from the ballads. One of the most remarkable of the popular lays chaunted about the streets of Norwich and Leeds in the time of Charles the Second, may still be read, as it is preserved in the British Museum. This ballad, which is described as "the vehement and bitter cry of labour against capital," tells of the "good old times when every artisan employed in the woolen manufacture lived as well as a farmer. But those times are past. Sixpence a day was now all that could be earned by hard labour at the loom. If the poor complained that they could not live on such a pittance, they were told that they were free to take it or leave it. For so miserable a recompense were the producers of wealth compelled to toil, rising early and lying down late, while the master clothier, eating, sleeping, and idling, became rich by their exertions."

It may be remarked here, that the ballad is really the battle hymn of the Hathnaughts. In all ages, in rude verse, the Hathnaughts have poured out their souls in complaints against the bitter and unequal struggle for existence, and a history of this ballad influence on the thought of the humble would make an instructive and illuminating, as well as an entertaining, chapter in a history of the industrial life.

Macaulay has this reference to child labour: "It may here be noticed that the practice of setting children prematurely to work, a practice which the State, the legitimate protector of those who cannot protect themselves, has, in our time, wisely and humanely interdicted, prevailed in the seventeenth century to an extent which, when compared with the extent of the manufacturing system, seems almost incredible. At Norwich, the chief seat of the clothing trade, a little creature of six years old was thought fit for labour. Several writers of that time, and among them some who were considered as eminently benevolent, mention, with exultation, the fact that in that single city, boys and girls of very tender age created wealth exceeding what was necessary for their own subsistence by twelve thousand pounds a year. The more carefully we examine the history of the past, the more reason shall we find to dissent from those who imagine that our age has been fruitful of new social evils. The truth is that the evils are, with scarcely an exception, old. That which is new is the intelligence which discerns and the humanity which remedies them."

Let us commend this observation to amateur sociologists and moral tinkers of our time who would have us believe we are going to Hell so fast that the brakes won't work.

Pursuing the history of the Hathnaughts further, Macaulay says: "During several generations, the Commissioners of Greenwich Hospital have kept a register of the wages paid to different classes of workmen who have been employed in the repairs of the building. From this valuable record it appears that, in the course of a hundred and twenty years, the daily earnings of the bricklayer have risen from half a crown to

four and ten pence, those of the mason
from a crown to five and three pence,
those of the carpenter from half a crown
to five and five pence, and those of the
plumber from three shillings to five and
six pence.

"It seems clear, therefore, that the
wages of labour, estimated in money,
were, in 1685, not more than half of
what they now are; and there were few
articles important to the workingman
of which the price was not, in 1685, more
than half of what it now is. Beer was
undoubtedly much cheaper in that age
than at present. Meat was also cheaper,
but was still so dear that hundreds of
thousands of families scarcely knew the
taste of it."

In this connection he cites King's
"Natural and Political Conclusions," in
which, he says, it is roughly estimated
the common people of England in that
day numbered 880,000 families; of these
families, according to King, 440,000 ate
animal food twice a week. The remaining 440,000 ate it not at all or at most
not oftener than once a week. The majority, Macaulay says, lived on rye, bar-
ley, and oats. We may profitably com-
pare this with Froude's description of
the Hathnaughts in the preceding century.

Below the labourers, as in the present
day, was the class that could not live
without some aid from the parish. In
our own day we learn from British blue
books and economic writers, that one

Hathnaught in every thirty-seven in England and Wales receives some measure of relief from the funds, and that in London the ratio is one in thirty-two. In 1685, according to Gregory King, as cited by Macaulay, the number of inhabitants of England who received relief constituted one-fourth of the population.

"And this estimate," says Macaulay, "which all our respect for his authority will scarcely prevent us from calling extravagant, was pronounced by Davenant eminently judicious." King and Davenant estimated the paupers and beggars in 1696 to number 1,330,000, out of a population of 5,500,000, an amazing proportion.

Macaulay touches upon the difficulties of reaching markets owing to the wretched state of the means of transportation. "The market place which the rustic can now reach with his cart in an hour was, a hundred and sixty years ago, a day's journey from him," says Macaulay. "The street which now affords to the artisan, during the whole night, a secure, convenient, and a brilliantly-lighted walk was, a hundred and sixty years ago, so dark after sunset that he would not have been able to see his hand, so ill-paved that he would have run constant risk of breaking his neck, and so ill-watched that he would have been in imminent danger of being knocked down and plundered of his small earnings."

Macaulay draws attention at this point to the wretched state of medicine and surgery in that day, declaring that bricklayers and chimney sweepers of to-day who may be injured can have treatment in hospitals that great lords like Ormond could not purchase in the seventeenth century.

In those days, too, he observes, workmen and wives had the common experience of ill treatment. "The discipline of workshops, of schools, of private families, though not more efficient than at present, was infinitely harsher," he adds. "Masters, well born and bred, were in the habit of beating their servants. Pedagogues knew of no way of imparting knowledge but by beating their pupils. Husbands of decent station were not ashamed to beat their wives.

"The implacability of hostile factions was such as we can scarcely conceive. Whigs were disposed to murmur because Stafford was suffered to die without seeing his bowels burned before his face. Tories reviled and insulted Russell as his coach passed from the Tower to the scaffold in Lincoln's Inn Fields. As little mercy was shown by the populace to sufferers of a humbler rank. If an offender was put into the pillory, it was well if he escaped with life from the shower of brickbats and paving stones. If he was tied to the cart's tail the crowd pressed round him, imploring the hangman to give it the fellow well and make him howl.

"Gentlemen arranged parties of pleasure to Bridewell on court days, for the purpose of seeing the wretched women, who beat hemp there, whipped. A man pressed to death for refusing to plead, a woman burned for coining, excited less sympathy than is now felt for a galled horse or an overdriven ox."

Canting Englishmen of to-day who would have you believe their country the sole custodian of all the virtues, and their statesmen the high priests of civilization; who love to dilate upon the horrors of life under the Roman Empire, and of the cruelties of the Reign of Terror during the French Revolution, can find plenty of parallels to these in their own country. We are told by various authorities that about 70,000 persons were executed during the reign of Henry VIII, including two of the old monster's wives, and it would not be hard to prove that more people suffered death in England for trivial offences than met a like fate during the whole course of the French Revolution.

"Woe to the man," says Rousseau in his "Political Economy," which forms part of the literature of the French Revolution, "who has a pretty daughter and a powerful neighbour." The same was true of Merrie England for many ages and even down to our time. Fielding's "Tom Jones," in the person of Molly Seagrim, shows us that the peasant's daughter was regarded as a morsel for the gentry, and Mrs. Lynn Linton, in

an article on George Eliot in a work
called "Women Novelists of the Reign
of Victoria," declares that even down
to her own day it was common for peasant girls to have children by the squire's
son, and such children were not frowned
upon as they are in our more enlightened twentieth century.

Sports of England up to a recent date
were brutal in the extreme, and ancient
Rome scarcely surpassed them in cruelty.
Macaulay declares that in the seventeenth
century, "multitudes assembled to see
gladiators hack each other to pieces with
deadly weapons, and shouted with delight
when one of the combatants lost a fin-
ger or an eye."

"The prisons," he continues, "were hells
on earth, seminaries of every crime and
of every disease. At the assizes the
lean and yellow culprits brought with
them from their cells to the dock an
atmosphere of stench and pestilence
which sometimes avenged them signally
on the bench, bar, and jury. But on all
this misery society looked with profound
indifference. Nowhere could be found
that sensitive and restless compassion
which has, in our time, extended a powerful protection to the factory child, to
the Hindoo widow, to the negro slave,
which pries into the stores and water-
casks of every emigrant ship, which
winces at every lash laid on the back
of a drunken soldier, which will not
suffer the thief in the hulks to be ill-fed
or overworked, and which has repeatedly

endeavoured to save the life even of a murderer."

Here we see the ceaseless and inevitable working out of the laws of progress—the softening of human emotions as we get further and further from the jungle and nearer and nearer the Age of Service, when men shall clasp hands as brothers, and work together for the common good. All honour to the noble Englishmen who have laboured for the new order, and who at this very moment in the British Parliament, the greatest stronghold of Privilege, are doing a mighty work for human freedom.

CHAPTER XII.

DENNIS AND THE INDUSTRIAL REVOLUTION.

In the annals of progress the eigh-teenth century might be called the Kindergarten of the Future, for it was a hundred years of the sowing of new ideas that it will take other centuries to reap and garner.

It is always a temptation to those that write of this fascinating age to discourse upon the progress of manners—the coarseness and vulgarity of the life and speech of the higher classes; the lack of refinement even in the clergy; the pursuit of women by the rakes and beaux of the times; the practical joking of the men about town; the dangers of streets and highways because of the numerous bands of Mohocks and highwaymen; the heavy hand of justice upon even the lightest offences which could send little children to the scaffold for the pettiest kind of petty larcenies; the horrors and promiscuity of prison life that huddled murderers, highwaymen, harlots, poor debtors, and even women and children, together, without a thought of the danger of contamination or caring for the

physical or spiritual comfort of the unfortunates.

It was an age of high swearing, gam-
bling, drunkenness, duelling, and indul-
gence in brutish sports.   The   country
squire as a rule had the manners of a
prize fighter, and the mass of the people
lived in misery and degradation.

Yet it was essentially an age of ideas,
when men of all classes were revolting
against the standards of their times. It
is because of this revolt and the ideas
scattered by the social insurgents that
we no longer have Squire Westerns, Parson Trullibers, imprisonment for   debt,
private madhouses, where it was easy to
incarcerate inconvenient relatives   who
were slow in dying, or streets so dangerous that a Sir Roger De Coverley must
needs provide himself with a body-guard
when he goes to a place of entertainment.

Its close was marked by the successful issue of the American and   French
Revolutions, and by a demand for political rights on the part of the British people that is working out the present economic destiny of the United Kingdom.
But, from the viewpoint of the Hathnaughts, the most interesting and significant event of the Eighteenth Century
was the Industrial Revolution, when domestic labour began to be replaced by
the factory system and machinery.

Like all things worth while, the Industrial Revolution was not conceived by
some genius over night and put in full

force the next morning. It was of slow growth, going back, indeed, to the third Edward, whom Hallam (Middle Ages) calls the father of English commerce. It was this Edward who, in 1331, "took advantage of the discontent among the manufacturers of Flanders to invite them as settlers into his dominions," according to Hallam. It was during this reign, too, Hallam tells us, that industry acquired a measure of respect, so that a merchant got on a footing somewhat equal to that of a landed proprietor. This change had an important effect on the matter of dress.

"By the Statute of Appeal in 37 Edward III," Hallam observes, "merchants and artificers who had five hundred pounds' value in goods and chattels might use the same dress as squires of one hundred pounds a year. All those who were worth more than this might dress like men of double that estate."

It is a safe wager that this law boomed the tailoring business, for it is not in human nature to resist the temptation to climb socially, especially when a king deigns to give you a friendly boost.

In Arnold Toynbee's "Industrial Revolution," we trace the development of the factory system in England. In a chapter on "Manufactures and Trades" he deals with the history of the woolen, iron, cotton, hardware, and hosiery trades in eighteenth-century England. The woolen trade, he says, probably existed in England from an early date, and he notes a mention of it in a law of 1224.

"In 1331," observes Toynbee, following Hallam, "John Kennedy brought the art of weaving woolen cloth from Flanders into England, and received the protection of the king, who at the same time invited over fullers and dyers. There is extant a petition of the worsted weavers and merchants of Norwich to Edward III in 1348. . . . In 1402 the manufacture was settled to a great extent in and near London, but it gradually shifted, owing to the high price of labour and provisions to Surrey, Kent, Essex, Berkshire, and Oxfordshire, and afterward still further into the counties of Dorset, Wilts, Somerset, Gloucester, and even as far as Yorkshire."

The cotton trade had so insignificant a beginning in England, according to Toynbee, as to be mentioned only once, and that incidentally, by Adam Smith. It was confined to Lancashire, where its headquarters were Manchester and Bolton. In 1760 not more than 40,000 persons were engaged in it.

Toynbee finds the hardware trade growing up about Sheffield and Birmingham, the latter town employing more than 50,000 in that industry in 1727.

The hosiery trade, too, Toynbee, declares, was in its infancy in the eighteenth century. By 1800 the manufacture of silk hosiery had centred in Derby, woolen hosiery in Leicester, though Nottingham had not yet absorbed the cotton hosiery trade. At the beginning of the century there were 14,000 looms in all the British islands.

Linen, he notes, was an ancient manufacture in England, and had been introduced into Dundee in the seventeenth century. It was the chief manufacture of Ireland, where it had been introduced by French Huguenots, who had settled there at the end of the seventeenth century.

"The machines used in the cotton manufacture," says Baines, in his "History of the Cotton Manufacture," as quoted by Toynbee, "were up to the year 1760 nearly as simple as those of India; though the loom was more strongly and perfectly constructed, and cards for combing the cotton had been adopted from the woolen manufacture, none but the strong cottons such as fustian and dimities were as yet made in England, and for these the demand must always have been limited."

"In 1738," Toynbee adds, "John Wyatt invented spinning by rollers, but the discovery never proved profitable. In 1760 the manufacturer of Lancashire began to use the flag shuttle. Calico printing was already largely developed.

"The reason why division of labour was carried out to so small an extent and invention so rare and so little regarded, is given by Adam Smith himself. Division of labour, as he points out, is limited by the extent of the market, and owing to bad means of communication the market for English manufactures was still a very narrow one. Yet England, however slow the development of her manufactures, advanced, nevertheless, more rapidly in

this respect than other nations.   One
great secret of her progress lay in the
facilities for water carriage afforded by
her rivers, for all communication by land
was still in the most neglected condition.
A second cause was the absence of internal customs barriers such as existed
in France and in Prussia until Stein's
time.   The home trade of England was
absolutely free. . . .

"When we turn to investigate the industrial organization of the time we find
that the class of capitalist employers was
as yet but in its infancy.   A large part
of our goods were still produced on the
domestic system.   Manufactures were little concentrated in towns, and only par-
tially separated from agriculture.   The
manufacturer was literally the man who
worked with his own hands in his own
cottage.   Nearly the whole cloth trade of
the West Riding, for instance, was organized on this system at the beginning
of the century.

"An important feature in the industrial organization of the time was the existence of a number of small master-man-
ufacturers, who were entirely independent, having capital and land of their own,
for they combined the culture of small
freehold pasture-farms with their handicraft.   Defoe (Defoe's Tour) has left an
interesting picture of their life.

"This system, however, was no longer
universal in Arthur Young's time (Northern Tour).   That writer found at Sheffield a silk-mill employing one hundred

and fifty-two hands, including women and children; at Darlington, one master-manufacturer employed above fifty looms; at Boynton there were one hundred and fifty hands in one factory.

"So, too, in the west of England cloth-trade the germs of the capitalist system were visible. The rich merchant gave out work to labourers in the surrounding villages, who were his employees, and were not independent. In the Nottingham hosiery trade there were in 1750 fifty manufacturers known as putters-out who employed twelve hundred frames; in Leicestershire eighteen hundred frames were so employed. In the hand-made nail business of Staffordshire and Worcestershire the merchant had warehouses in different parts of the district, and gave out nail rods to the nail-master sufficient for a week's work for him and his family.

"In Lancashire we can trace step by step the growth of the capitalist employer. At first we see, as in Yorkshire, the weaver furnishing himself with warp and weft, which he worked up in his own house and brought himself to market. By degrees he found it difficult to get yarn from the spinners; so the merchants at Manchester gave him out linen warp and raw cotton, and the weaver became dependent on them. Finally the merchant would get together thirty or forty looms in a town. This was the nearest approach to the capitalist system before the great mechanical inventions."

Toynbee describes the great fairs, where a large part of the inland traffic was carried on, and which were still almost as important as in the Middle Ages. The most famous of all was the fair at Sturbridge, to which goods were brought on pack-horses. There were also great fairs at Lynn, Boston, Gainsborough, and Beverly.

In ancient Rome (Fowler's Social Life at Rome in the Age of Cicero) there was a good banking system, conducted by the Argentarii. The Argentarius took money for deposit on interest, and there were bills of exchange, letters of credit, and something conforming to our check. Yet in the Middle Ages merchants and manufacturers were hampered by the absence of banks and a good system of exchange. Even in the eighteenth century ready cash was essential, for banking, Toynbee says, was little developed. "The Bank of England existed," he continues, "but before 1759 issued no notes of less value than twenty pounds. By a law of 1709, no other bank of more than six partners was allowed; and in 1750, according to Burke, there were not more than twelve bankers' shops out of London. The Clearing House was not established till 1775."

So isolated were some districts that at the beginning of the nineteenth century the Yorkshire yeoman, according to Robert Southey, as told in "The Doctor" and quoted by Toynbee, was ignorant of sugar, potatoes, and cotton, and the Cumberland dalesman, as appears in Wordsworth's "Guide to the Lakes," lived entirely on the produce of his farm.

"It was the domestic system," says Toynbee, "which the great Socialist writers, Sismondi and Lassalle, had in their minds when they inveighed against the modern organization of industry. Those who lived under it, they pointed out, though poor, were on the whole prosperous; over-production was absolutely impossible."

What is true of England is true of the beginnings of trade everywhere. But what a change had been wrought in the time of Napoleon, when British trade had developed to such an extent that the Corsican bandit referred to the tight little island as a "nation of shopkeepers."

Since the beginning of the nineteenth century the invention of labour-saving machinery has completely revolutionized manufacturing industries, not only in England, but throughout the world. These inventions, which have proved great blessings to labour, have always been fought by the Hathnaughts, particularly trades-unionists, and even in our own day labour-saving devices and implements are as bitterly opposed as in the days of Arkwright and the spinning jenny.

This hostile attitude of ignorant labour toward the very implements that are hastening the day of proletarian emancipation, is well set forth in Charles Reade's novel "Put Yourself in His Place." In this work we see the violent opposition that met Henry Little's experiments with inventions, even to the extent of endangering life and property, something after the manner of the MacNamaras of our own times. One great result of the introduction of machinery and the development of science has been to diversify labour. There are to-day many hundreds of different ways of making a living that were not known in Shakespeare's day. Even such a simple thing as the souvenir post card gives work to thousands.

It is a disputed question, however, among economists whether the Industrial Revolution has been an unmixed blessing to labour. There seems to be a law, as John G. Lockhart points out in his "History of Napoleon Buonaparte," commenting upon the effects of the French Revolution and of Napoleon's career upon the world, "that violent and sudden changes in the structure of social and political order have never yet occurred without inflicting utter misery upon at least one generation."

The Industrial Revolution had its tragedies. Before the enactment of the Factory Acts, the Hathnaughts, men, women, and children, were at the mercy of unscrupulous capitalists. Gibbins, in his "Industrial History of England," declares that it was "not until the wages of the workmen had been reduced to a starvation level that they consented to their children and wives being employed in the mills." To get labour the greedy mill-owners, under the smug pretence of apprenticing them to the new employments, obtained children from the parish workhouses, whom they never paid, and who worked long hours, day and night, underfed and ill-treated. These children slept in relays in beds that never had a chance to cool, and such as showed a disposition to run away, worked and slept with irons riveted on their ankles, and with long links reaching to the hips.

Gibbins quotes his authorities for these statements and shows the sexes living promiscuously and with less decorum than the brutes. This trade in workhouse children became in time a regular slave traffic. There are still traces of it in the world, but enlightened legislation nowadays tends to humanize the Industrial Life and checks the martyrdom of childhood.

Karl Marx, in his "Capital," discussing this awful traffic in child labour in England, says that the hapless apprentices were flogged, tortured, and fettered, and that this squeezing of profits out of human blood continued until Sir Robert Peel introduced a bill for the protection of children. In the view of Marx, Capital came into the world, dripping from head to foot and from every pore with blood and dirt. This is, of course, the extreme view of the militant Socialist, and is unfair to the progressive and conscientious Capitalist, who from the first has not been neglectful of the rights and comforts of his employees. Sir Robert Peel was himself a capitalist.

CHAPTER XIII.

JACQUES BONHOMME, FRENCH HATHNAUGHT.

"Jacques Bonhomme has a broad back and can stand it," was a stock phrase of the nobility and clergy of the ancient régime in France, when adding an additional burden to the already intolerable load carried by the French Hathnaught.

Feudalism, we have seen in previous chapters and from citations drawn from Buckle, Duruy, and Bonnemere, was always stronger in France than elsewhere because of the power of the nobles to enforce their claims even against the kings. In all the tribe of Hathnaught, no one had less than poor Jacques Bonhomme. Temporary concessions or recognition of his class as a third estate, as in the time of Philip, the Fair who, in 1302, called together the States General of nobles, clergy and commons, were short lived. Men like Etienne Marcel tried in vain to improve conditions, and despair often took the form of terrible risings and reprisals such as that of the Jacquerie or Hathnaughts in 1358, but all ended in the further enslavement of the common herd.

Some towns, notably Laon, had wrung charters from the king, nobles and clergy, but these communal experiments were ill-starred, and after a brief blaze of glory, sank back into the general mass of degradation which tyranny attempted to make the fixed, permanent and unalterable condition of life. Poor Jacques staggered on beneath his burden, worn to a rail and little better than skin and bone, paying all the taxes and reaping none of the benefits, while nobles and clergy, made more insolent with the passing years, waxed fatter and fatter.

Jacques carried this crushing weight for more than four hundred years after the rising of the Jacquerie until, in 1789, the oppressed and despoiled Hathnaughts burst all bounds and feudalism and privilege disappeared in a torrent of the sublimest rage that this world has ever known—the immortal French Revolution.

The literature of this Revolution is immense and is still growing. As time passes and passions subside, men are coming to see the beneficial results to the world of this outpouring of a nation's wrath beside which the wrath of Achilles was the wail of an infant in the midst of a cannonading.

Carlyle's celebrated work on the period must not be regarded as authoritative. It is a great prose epic, full of power and brilliancy, but if you know little of history to start with you will gain little knowledge from Carlyle of the causes and effects of this mighty upheaval. It bears the same relation to other and more judicious works on the Revolution that Worcestershire sauce does to a steak, and if taken in this way it is very appetizing.

To mention authorities would be to print an immense bibliography. Important works bearing upon the subject have been produced by Taine, DeTocqueville, Thiers, Blanc, Van Laun, Lamartine, Rocquain, Arthur Young (Travels in France During the Years 1787, 1788, 1789), Mignet, Doniol, Michelet, Alison, Sybel, Hausser, Rabaut, Buchez, Kerverseau and Clavelin, Ternaux, Madame de Stael, Janet, Burke, Quinet, Berriat, Mackintosh, and Croker. Dickens' "Tale of Two Cities" is a study of the period in fiction.

When the Revolution broke out, liberty had entirely disappeared and the Hathnaughts were oppressed, impoverished, and threatened with starvation. They lived in poor cabins, their clothing hardly deserved the name of rags, and their main article of diet was black bread, with a substitute for tea made by pouring water over husks. To possess white bread and be discovered, meant a visitation from the tax-collector. Every tax pressed down upon the poor and industrious, while the rich, idle rascals, and clergy were immune.

Some of the worst burdens were the taille, a land tax, the gabelle or salt tax; tithes of various kinds, for an idle, vicious, and worthless clergy had to get

its pound of flesh also; wine and poll
taxes and seigneurial dues; corvees or
forced, unpaid labour on the highways
during a quarter of the year, for the
roads had to be kept in good condition
for the coaches of the lazy and rascally
nobles.

Rousseau in his "Political Economy,"
contending that the law should reflect
the popular will, and that there should
be no privileged classes with extremes of
poverty and riches, says: "If a man of
position robs his creditors or commits
other acts of rascality, is he not sure of
impunity? Are not all the blows he dis-
tributes, all the violences he commits,
the very murders and assassinations of
which he is guilty, hushed up and forgotten in a few months? But let this
man himself be robbed, and the whole
police set to work, and woe to the poor
innocent man whom they suspect. If he
has to pass a dangerous place, escorts
scour the country. If a noise is made at
his gate, at a word all is silent. If the
axle of his coach breaks, everybody runs
to help him. If a carter crosses his path
his attendants are ready to knock him
down, while fifty decent pedestrians going to business might be crushed rather
than a lazy rascal be stopped in his
coach.

"All these attentions do not cost him
a sou; they are the rights that belong to
the rich man. How different with the
poor. The more he needs humanity, the
more society refuses it to him. If there
are corvees to make, recruits required, it

is he who has the preference. He always bears besides his own burdens, those from which his rich neighbour is exempt."

Old people were compelled to beat ponds at night so that the favoured families might not have their slumbers disturbed by the croaking of frogs. The poor tiller of the soil had no redress if his lord's pigeons consumed his grain; indeed, it is not unlikely that if he interfered with those birds which he was precluded by law from possessing, he might have been subjected to punishment. His lord while hunting had a perfect right to pull down the fences and ride over his crops.

If a man high in favour at Court wished to get rid of an enemy he had the means of doing so through the lettre de cachet, and the enemy was hastened to the Bastile without formality of trial or even the merits of the case being given consideration.

Voltaire once served a term of imprisonment for merely resenting verbally a wanton insult from a Court parasite. We may be sure that incidents like this made the little man of Ferney do yeoman service in bringing on the Revolution.

Court favourites and royal mistresses received pensions and gifts which taxed the Hathnaughts beyond the limits of endurance. Camille Desmoulins, one of the leaders of the Revolution, speaking of one Ducrot, who was in receipt of a pension of seventeen hundred livres for his ser-

vices as hairdresser to Mademoiselle
d'Artois, observed that the young lady
"died at the age of three before she had
any hair."

Arthur Young, whose "Travels" are a
mine of information on the state of the
country before the Revolution, speaks of
the enormous revenues (300,000 livres a
year) of the Abbot of the Benedictine
Abbey of St. Germain, and noting how
the land was wasted, declares that one-
fourth the sum would establish a noble
farm. The "fat ecclesiastic," as Young
calls him, like the rest of his tribe, did
nothing to improve the condition of
the wretched people. "Fat ecclesiastic"!
How often that characterization appears
in the writings of those who have touched upon the history of the Hathnaughts
across the ages. We have been kept
lean while monks and prelates are known
by their anatomical architecture—the ro-
tundity of their convex facades.

Another observation of Young is significant and worthy of chronicle. He
found that the great seignior, Conde, had
more than a hundred square miles of
idle land and forest which teemed with
game. Yet the poor inhabitants might
not till any of this land nor could the
Hathnaughts destroy even the meanest
of the game that kept on increasing and
pestered the poor dwellers in the neighbourhood to the limit of endurance.

All burdens fell upon the shoulders of
men of ignoble birth. Members of the
tribe of Hathnaught might never aspire

to preferment in the church, the army or the State. Only persons of rank were entitled to own pigeons. In consequence of this systematic degradation of the people there was little mechanical skill or real progress, and all departments requiring such talents were in the hands of foreigners. Manufactures were encouraged only so far as they contributed to the luxury or comfort of the nobility. None of the blessings of modern liberty— a free press, free speech, and open discussion, the suffrage, representation and the popular voice in government, trial by jury, and the habeas corpus, were known. You could tell one's rank instantly from his dress or deportment. It was only just before the Revolution that the establishment of clubs broke down barriers sufficiently to enable educated men to come together without the ancient, aristocratic distinction of rank.

That even the most sacred tie in the world, the intimacy of a good man and a good woman, bound together by marriage, was not respected, is illustrated in a story told by Buckle in his "History of Civilization."

"In the middle of the eighteenth century," he says, "there was an actress on the French stage of the name of Chantilly. She, though beloved by Maurice de Saxe, preferred a more honourable attachment, and married Favart, the well-known writer of songs and of comic operas. Maurice, amazed at her boldness, applied for aid to the French crown. That he should have made such an application is sufficiently strange; but the result of it is hardly to be paralleled except in some Eastern despotism. The government of France, on hearing the circumstance, had the inconceivable baseness to issue an order directing Favart to abandon his wife, and intrust her to the charge of Maurice, to whose embraces she was compelled to submit."

A sense of humour impels us to one more citation, this time from Taine's "Ancient Régime." It is his famous account of the progress of the French King from the moment he arises in the morning, through all the intricacies of getting him into his shirt and down to the antechamber where visiting grandees await him. It is that consummate ass, Louis XIV, of whom he speaks:

"In the morning at the hour named by himself beforehand, the head valet awakens him; five series of persons enter in turn to perform their duty, and, 'although very large, there are days when the waiting rooms can hardly contain the crowd of courtiers.' "

Scores of officials and servitors tackled the king from different angles, each with a special job—spirits of wine were poured on the king's hands from a service of plate, and he was then handed a basin of holy water—this old roue with a palaceful of mistresses. He crossed himself and said a prayer, which no doubt the fools about him thought was taken down in shorthand by an angel. In presence of

every one his Majesty got out of bed
and put on his slippers. He received his
dressing gown from the grand chamberlain and the first gentleman, and sat
him down in a chair in which later he
would put on his clothes.

Then another group of persons, each
with a distinct duty, came in and danced
attendance on Louis. All sorts of tom-
fool things followed before the king
washed his hands preparatory to dressing. Two pages—count 'em, as Tody
Hamilton, Barnum's press agent, would
say—removed the royal slippers. The
grand master of the wardrobe drew off
the royal nightshirt by the right hand
and the first valet of the wardrobe did
the same to the left, while both officials
handed the garment to an officer of the
wardrobe. Then came a valet of the
wardrobe in solemn manner bearing the
shirt of his Majesty, wrapped in white
taffeta.

Does his Majesty slip into his shirt
without further ado? Nothing of the
sort; he is far from getting into it yet.
"The honour of handing it," says Taine,
"is reserved to the sons and grandsons
of France; in default of these, to the
princes of the blood or those legitimated;
in their default to the grand chamberlain
or to the first gentleman of the bed-
chamber—the latter case, it must be observed, being very rare, the princes being
obliged to be present at the king's lever
as well as the princesses at that of the
Queen. At last the shirt is presented,

and a valet carries off the old one; the first valet of the wardrobe and the first valet-de-chambre hold the fresh one, each by a right and left arm, respectively; while two other valets during this operation extend his dressing gown in front of him to serve as a screen. The shirt is now on his back, and the toilet commences."

Louis is still far from dressed, but the reader who would know more of the details will have to consult Taine. Enough has been shown to prove that the useless, wasteful, and criminal expenditures of this corrupt Court for a day, would support half a province of Hathnaughts. And the peasantry had to furnish the wherewithal in the sweat of their brows.

Contrast all this with the simple and artless grace of our old friend Martin Gilhooly, the brick-layer, who bounds out of bed in the morning, yanks off his cutty sark without ceremony and jumps into his simple articles of attire, while in the kitchen his good wife Mary Ann is slipping a modest repast into his dinner-pail. Twenty minutes after Martin awakes, he is on his way to the scene of his labour. And Martin does a better day's work than Louis ever did, the best day he ever knew.

CHAPTER XIV.

DENNIS, THE PLOUGHMAN, IN POLITICS.

It is a temperamental difference of character that makes the British Hathnaught gain concessions from the ruling caste by agitation, mass meeting and petition, that his French cousin thinks impossible of attainment save when demanded back of a barricade.

In the last hundred years the Hathnaughts have seen some mighty changes, notable among them being the removal of the civil and other disabilities of the Catholics and Jews; the great Reform bill of 1832, which dealt a deathblow to aristocratic privilege and ascendency; the repeal of the odious Corn Laws in 1846, establishing free trade as a natural right, and reducing the high cost of living; further parliamentary reform in 1866; disestablishment of the Irish Church and the abolishing of the tithe system which made the mass of the Irish people support a small body of ecclesiastics whose religion they despised.

But for the purposes of the present discussion the most significant reform was that which in 1884 extended the franchise to the agricultural labourers, the Hathnaughts of rural Britain, who, up to that time, had advanced but little beyond the serfdom of the Middle Ages. This bill swelled the voting lists by a round two million.

It is not exaggeration to say that in the middle of the nineteenth century there was not a more wretched or hopeless class of Hathnaughts in the world than the English agricultural labourers. Mr. Warren Isham, in "The Mud Cabin," a study of the character and tendencies of British institutions (D. Appleton & Co., 1853), records some first hand investigations of this unfortunate class. He found an absolute lack of interest in the tenant and labourer on the part of Lord Have-and-Hold, who fattened on his ill-gotten part of poor Hathnaught's earnings.

"It is enough for him to know," says Mr. Isham, "that if they die of destitution, there are enough others to take their places and labour for the same pittance."

There is evidence that this indifference to the comforts of the labourer still characterizes the British landlord. Mrs. Philip Snowden, in an address delivered some years ago at the Brooklyn Academy of Music, declared that although he was at the head of the sanitary reform commission, the Duke of Northumberland opposed sanitary legislation because it would materially increase his own obligations. Mrs. Snowden told of twenty-eight thousand tenements inspected, only one hundred and twenty-eight of which had bathroom facilities.

The workhouse has always been the British landlord's solution of the question of Hathnaught's miseries. Mr. Isham found that in Dorsetshire it cost twenty-seven pounds 9s. 9d. annually to support a prisoner. Agricultural labourers did not earn more than twenty pounds. A single criminal cost more to support than an entire family often numbering five, six or eight children.

"Is it a wonder," asks Mr. Isham, "that the famished wretch should be a thief, schooled to it as he is by the robbery practiced upon himself, and goaded to it by the pinchings of hunger? But though that be his name, and though, to expiate his offence, he be sent to Botany Bay, he has cleaner hands and a lighter load of guilt on his soul than tne landlord who stays behind to riot upon the fruit of his earnings."

About the same time Mr. Isham was making his study of British industry so far as it applies to the agricultural labourer, the London Morning Chronicle was publishing the results of an investigation conducted by its own commissioner. "Education," said the Chronicle, "has advanced him but little beyona wnat he was in the days of William the Conqueror. As he was in generations gone by, so he is now, a moral enigma, a physical scandal, an intellectual cataleptic." This writer declares, "They are entirely wanting in the independent bearing of the man, are awkward in their gait, and dress in a garb which belongs to another century than this."

Isham says that of the marriages that transpired in England and Wales in 1839, 1840, 1841, out of 367,894 couples united in wedlock, 122,457 men and 181,378 women made their marks in the register. He saw whole troops of females at work in the field, toiling at the spade, the mattock, and the hoe. Higher education for these people was opposed on the ground that it would make the Hathnaughts look above their station and there would be no one to black the boots or tend the horses of the gentry.

Isham contends that the landlord, and not the Hathnaughts, benefited principally by the abolition of serfdom. At the exhibition of the "Works of Industry of All Nations," held in England in 1852, he saw one thousand Hathnaughts in their smock frocks and with red ribbons on their hats marched two by two into the Crystal Palace as though on purpose for a show.

These men spoke to Isham of belonging to this squire or that lord, and an Englishman of intelligence standing by told him they belonged to the soil as much as the serfs of Russia, and, although not named in the bond, were actually transferred with the soil from master to master.

Citing Hallam's "Middle Ages" as authority, Isham continues: "No more than three centuries ago, the forefathers of those people were serfs, which is but another name for slaves. They were bought and sold, not only with the soil, but without the soil, and were subject to the lash. Between the landlord and the serfs stood the vassal, who sustained much the same relation to each as the tenant farmer does now; that is, the landlord let out the land and serfs to the vassal, as he does now the land to the tenant farmer, the labourers, though not actually stipulated for, continuing to sustain much the same relation to both as the serfs did before. The appearance, the legal forms of serfdom have been abolished, I am bold to say, the better to enjoy the reality."

There is very strong evidence that the landlord has gained by the change from serfdom to the present system, for he is relieved of the old feudal responsibility of furnishing his quota of men for military service, and of caring for his serfs when ill or incapacitated. The London Morning Chronicle, which made its investigation about the same time Isham did, quoted Fortesque to prove that four hundred years ago the principal food of the serfs was meat. Harrison's "Description of England" has a like observation. "The Spanish nobles who came into England with Philip," says Harrison, "were astonished at the diet which they found among the poor. 'These English,' said one of them, 'have their houses made of sticks and dirt, but they fare commonly as well as the King.' "

We are told by Isham that there was an understanding among the farmers of a parish that they would not employ each other's labourers, an understanding so well observed that a Hathnaught, fired by a sense of liberty and setting out upon his travels to better his fortune, met, at the first place he asked for employment, the question that always put a damper upon his hopes and sent him back to his old servitude: "Why did you leave your master?" This is what the Englishman meant when he told Isham that the Hathnaughts were still transferred with the soil as in the days of serfdom.

Serfdom is not without its friends among modern historians. That high Tory, Sir Archibald Alison, in his "History of Europe" (Vol. 4; Harper & Brothers, 1843), says in a footnote on page twelve after quoting Cochrane's "Travels in Russia and Siberia": "It would be a happy day for the Irish peasantry, the slaves of their own heedless and savage passions, when they exchanged places with the Siberian convicts, subjected to the less grievous yoke of punishment and despotism."

In the main body of the text this "amiable" historian says: "It would be a real blessing to its (Ireland's) inhabitants, in lieu of the destitution of freedom, to obtain the protection of slavery." As a "Modest Proposal" this beats Swift's suggestion to use children for food in Ireland, but there is this difference— the heavy-minded old Tory, Alison, was in earnest; Swift was only fooling.

Duruy in his "Middle Ages" makes particular note of the modern champions of serfdom and cites their stock arguments. One Ditchfield, in a recent work entitled "The Old English Squire," mourns the passing of this dominant class and bewails the fact that the auctioneer's hammer is heard everywhere throughout the land. Yet to those who look forward to a day of freedom for the English Hathnaught, this sound may verily be compared to the music of a liberty bell. It is no longer possible, as Bulwer Lytton shows it was in his romance, "My Novel," for Squire Hazeldean to put Hathnaught in the stocks, and, thanks to the good work accomplished since the days of Joseph Arch, the English agricultural labourer is assuming more of the manner and erect stature of a freeman.

Joseph Arch was one of those simple souls that appear from time to time across the ages, who are born with a mission, and have the divine call to preach. Justin McCarthy tells his story in "A History of Our Own Times." He says: "Suddenly in the spring of 1872, not long after the opening of Parliament, vague rumours began to reach London of a movement of some kind among the labourers of South Warwickshire. It was first reported that they had asked for an increase of wages; then that they were actually forming a labourers' union, after the pattern of the artisans; then that they were on strike. There came accounts of meetings of rural labourers —meetings positively where men made speeches. Instantly the London papers sent down their special correspondents, and for weeks the movement among the agricultural labourers of South Warwickshire—the county of Shakespeare—became the sensation of London.

"How the thing first came about is not very clear. But it seems that in one of the South Warwickshire villages, where there was sad and sullen talk of starvation, it occurred to some one to suggest a strike against the landlords. The thing took fire somehow. A few men accepted it at once. In the neighbouring village was a man who, although only a day labourer, had been long accustomed to act as a volunteer preacher of Methodism, and who, by his superior intelligence, his good character, and his effective way of talking, had acquired a great influence among his fellows. This man was Joseph Arch. He was consulted, and he approved of the notion. He was asked if he would get together a meeting and make a speech, and he consented.

"Calling a meeting of day labourers then was almost as bold a step as proclaiming a revolution. Yet it was done somehow. There were no circulars, no placards, none of the machinery which

we associate with the getting up of a
meeting. The news had to be passed on
by word of mouth that a meeting was
to be held and where; the incredulous
had to be convinced that there was really
to be a meeting; the timid had to be
prevailed upon to take courage and go.
The meeting was held under a great
chestnut tree, which thereby acquired a
sort of fame. There a thousand labourers came together and were addressed
by Joseph Arch. He carried them all
with him. His one great idea—great
and bold to them, simple and small to
us—was to form a labourers' union like
the trades-unions of the cities. The idea
was taken up with enthusiasm. New
branches were formed every day. Arch
kept on holding meetings and addressing
crowds."

When the movement was in full
swing, important men like Auberon Herbert lent it their support and Arch became associated with members of Parliament and others of a class unfamiliar
to him, but McCarthy says his good
sense never forsook him. Many were
surprised to note that when the Hathnaughts showed political predilection
they inclined more toward Liberalism
than they did toward Toryism. "Most
persons," says McCarthy, "had supposed
that a race of beings brought up for
generations under the exclusive tutor-
ship of the landlord, the vicar, and the
wives of the landlords and the vicar,
would have had any political tendencies

they possessed drilled and drummed into the grooves of Toryism."

It may be set down in passing that the Church of England, with its system of putting the livings or rectorships in the hands of the powerful families, and the resultant filling of these with complacent and pliable vicars, has had a vicious effect upon the development of the character of the humble. One little hymn of this church, the stronghold of the dominant class, chants the lovely thought that God has ordered the estate of the great and the lowly and that all should be content to let things remain as they are. But it is refreshing news to read in the press of the current day that there is a loud demand in England for the suppression of this canting ode of Smugdom. We return to McCarthy's history: "The landlords in most places declared themselves against the movement of the labourers. Some of them denounced it in unmeasured language. Mr. Disraeli at once sprang to the front as the champion of feudal aristocracy and the British country squire. The controversy was taken up in the House of Commons, and served, if it did nothing else, to draw all the more attention to the condition of the British labourer.

"One indirect but necessary result of the agitation was to remind the public of the injustice done to the rural population when they were left unfranchised at the time of the passing of the last Reform Bill. The injustice was strongly pressed upon the Government, and Mr. Gladstone frankly acknowledged that it would be impossible to allow things to remain long in their anomalous state. In truth, when the Reform Bill was passed nobody supposed that the rural population were capable of making any use of a vote. Therefore the movement which began in Warwickshire took two directions when the immediate effects of the partial strike were over. A permanent union of labourers was formed, corresponding generally in system with the organizations of the cities. The other direction was distinctly political. The rural population through their leaders joined with the reformers of the cities for the purpose of obtaining an equal franchise in town and country; in other words, for the enfranchisement of the peasantry. The emancipation of the rural labourers began when the first meeting answered the appeals of Joseph Arch. The rough and ready peasant preacher had probably little idea, when he made his speech under the chestnut tree, that he was speaking the first words of a new chapter of the country's history."

Arch afterward sat in Parliament as the first representative there of the tribe of Hathnaught.

CHAPTER XV.

THE RIGHT HON. DENNIS HATH-NAUGHT, M. P.

Permit me to introduce to you Mr. Dennis Hathnaught, M. P. You will hardly recognize him, but he is the same old fellow we saw in ancient days wearing an iron collar; toiling as serf in mediæval times; rising in insurrection under Wat Tyler, and finally organizing into unions under Joseph Arch. Now he has kicked over the conventions of ages by actually entering Parliament and taking his seat beside the scions of Have-and-Hold. The Labour party is becoming a power in politics and in Parliament.

When the House of Lords attacked the budget in 1910, the question of the right of the hereditary house, irresponsible to the people, to interfere with the financial legislation of the country, became acute and led to proposals for its abolition or its reformation along radical lines, such as curtailing its privileges, doing away with its power of veto, or making it an elective second chamber.

Lords of Have-and-Hold were not so obtuse that they did not realize the gravity of the situation, and so, in the election that followed the appeal to the country in 1910 they adopted the tactics of the Artful Dodger, who, although he was the thief himself, always tried to distract attention from himself by shouting "Stop thief" the loudest. The emissaries of the Lords succeeded very well in getting the Hathnaughts' edge off them by raising the cry for tariff reform, deriding the free-trade policy that has governed England since the Corn laws days, and demanding the establishment of a protective tariff, which they declared meant work and wages for Dennis. How these privileged gentlemen do worry about the work and wages of the proletariat—when they want his vote. The Lords, as a matter of fact, were simply stealing the thunder of Joseph Chamberlain, who came out, years before, in support of a return to the protective policy which had been shattered by Richard Cobden and the old Corn Laws agitators.

Chief of the Hathnaughts in Parliament is Lloyd George. His underlying idea of taxation is that it should be borne by those that can best afford to bear it. He holds that it should fall upon the superfluities of life, rather than upon the necessities. It is a revival of the old question that so long agitated France, and finally led to the Revolution. In the days of the old régime in France the rich food and luxuries of the rich were not taxed, but the bread and salt of the people were. The equipage of the rich noble was not burdened with a tax, but the donkey of the poor peddler and trades-

man was. In like manner, the English
Lords have been willing to put the burden of taxation on the back of poor Dennis. Lloyd George thinks there has come
a time in British history when Dennis
and milord should change burdens. He
contends that his reforms mean the setting up of a great insurance scheme for
the unemployed, the sick, and the infirm.
He is for the proletariat, so long exploited for the aggrandizement of the nobility.

The *Westminster Gazette,* supporting
Lloyd George, declared that England has
prolonged a feudal land system to the
point at which it seriously threatens the
further progress of the country. The
Lords and their kind have grown fat on
unearned increment. The land of England is owned by a smaller group of persons than a like area in any other part
of the globe. Half of England is possessed by two thousand five hundred persons. The Duke of Sutherland owns 1,-
358,600 acres. It is easy to see, therefore, that there is in Britain a great
landlord's trust, of which the House of
Lords may be called the Board of Direc-
tors.

Mr. G. K. Chesterton, who has done
yeoman service in the Hathnaught cause,
declares truly that great estates in the
hands of the few was one of the main
causes in bringing about the downfall of
Rome. He finds the system to be the
curse of Ireland and the cause of its
misery, and points out that the system

brought on the French Revolution. As a matter of fact, most of the great landlords of Great Britain and Ireland are the descendants of parasites and sycophants who got their estates as a reward for their fawning and cajoling of the great. In some few cases the properties were the reward of great services to the state, but these are the exception. Much sympathy has been wasted upon the poet Spenser, who wrote "The Faerie Queen," because his estate in Ireland was sacked by Irish rebels and his home burned. But Spenser, like others of his kind, was simply a receiver of stolen goods. His Irish property was unjustly wrested from a native of the soil and turned over to him as a reward for his glorification of Elizabeth. All the real good men of this stamp have ever conferred upon their country in a material way would fit snugly in the snuff box of a microbe.

It was the purpose of the land system proposed by Lloyd George to encourage the better use of the land by making large quantities of it available for homes, for industrial purposes, and for public enjoyment. Every owner of land was required to furnish an estimate of his property at his own valuation. This included the total value of property as it stood, with buildings and other improvements, and that of the site alone—the "original site value."

It was the starting point of a new system of taxation. It was planned to take, by taxation, part of the increased value of these lands, not due to any exertion of the landlord, but to the increasing growth and prosperity of the country—the unearned increment. Undeveloped land, which now bears lightly, the burden of taxation—hardly enough, in fact, to be appreciable—would have to assume its share of taxation.

This, Lloyd George and thinkers in the same economic school contend, will force landlords to put the land without delay to its "most socially advantageous use," to quote the Manchester *Guardian,* one of the great provincial newspapers of England. The great world war has stopped all progressive legislation, but the new Doomsday Survey of England is simply postponed, for the democratic movement has too much impetus to go back now.

Expropriation of the landlords by state purchase, on a plan similar to that now being worked out in Ireland, has been suggested for Great Britain, but on this point Lloyd George said: "If the extravagant prices which have hitherto accompanied every acquisition of land for public or industrial purposes are to rule in future, the peasant proprietary is doomed to a subsidized insolvency." When he first urged a new state valuation, the Conservatives denounced it as virtual confiscation.

Lloyd George and the party of Hathnaughts wish to do away with land monopoly, so that rural England can be recreated and developed. They mean to put an end to the holding of vast areas, over which the idle rich, when making holiday, may hunt a poor fox or deer to its death. The new order of things means the passing of the old-fashioned country gentleman, who rules like a lord of feudal days, tyrannizing over a tenantry doomed for lack of opportunity to a poverty that is hopeless. The gentry in many instances hold the parish living, to which they assign a clergyman who can be depended upon to preach the gospel of Christ according to the version of the landlord, and he also has the power in many instances to say who shall represent his district in the House of Commons. The rotten and pocket boroughs of England have not all disappeared, and the extension of the suffrage and the secret ballot does not always enable the Hathnaughts to vote according to their inclinations and consciences.

Mr. A. St. John Adcock, a London journalist and novelist, writing in the London *Daily Chronicle,* from personal observations made during the election following the lord's rejection of the budget in 1910, declared that the landlords dictated how the rural population should vote, and that the people were little more than serfs. We have seen by the career of Joseph Arch, who in 1872, after a hard-fought campaign against the low wages paid agricultural labourers, organized the National Agricultural Labourers' Union, that there is plenty of evidence of the survival of serfdom in rural England. Mr. Adcock said that the lords dominated

not only the land and the tenantry, but
the schools and the churches. He told
of one noble Duke who caused his mono-
gram to appear above the doors of the
cottages in a village he owned. His mon-
ogram also appeared on the outer wall of
the church, as if he were the local deity,
and the place were dedicated to his worship.

"The villagers," Mr. Adcock said, "are
the duke's tenants, and, since none of the
poorer dwellers hereabouts believe in the
secrecy of the ballot, it is easy to guess
for which candidate they voted, and
why."

These wretched Hathnaughts are forced
to vote against their own best interests
through fear of eviction, the blacklist,
and persecution. Even the school-chil-
dren, Mr. Adcock said, were forced to
wear the blue rosettes of the Conservative candidate, although they were the
sons and daughters of men Liberal by
conviction. A fine state of affairs in free
and merrie England. These people live
in wretched hovels, and their masters
make no effort, as shown by Mr. Adcock, to improve their condition or elevate
them in any way.

One of the worst types of landlords
in England is what is known as "the
ground landlord." Leaseholders may own
the buildings in a town, but some peer
may have an ancient title to the land, and
as a "ground landlord" exact tribute.

Vast areas of England are made soli-
tudes for sports, while thousands cry for

bread and a chance to work. To learn
how the lords use the idle land that it
is proposed to make productive through
taxation, take this illustration of the late
Mr. William T. Stead, the noted English
journalist, writing in the *Review of Reviews*, London. Mr. Stead took for his
purpose the estate of Strathfieldsaye, of
eight thousand acres, a grant to the Duke
of Wellington, as a reward for military
services. The birds and other game shot
by succeeding dukes and their friends
from 1887 to 1909, a period of twenty-
two years, including pheasants, par-
tridges, hares, rabbits, and woodcock,
numbered one hundred and forty-nine
thousand two hundred and eighty-five.
Farmers or Hathnaughts dare not touch
a single bird or game animal, even if
they find them on the road or upon their
own leased land, excepting by express
permission of the duke. To enter a preserve, Mr. Stead says, is to incur the suspicion of felony as a poacher or game
thief.

Prevented from spreading out upon the
land, the source of all wealth, the Hathnaughts are crowded into the towns and
cities, and there is frightful congestion
and incidental poverty. Pauperism is on
the increase, and there is a noticeable deterioration, physically, of the common
English people.

Figures give the number of paupers
in England and Wales as almost a million. This vast army, comprising one in
every thirty-seven of the population, is

receiving public relief in some form. A report of the Local Government Board in 1910 showed that the number of able-bodied men relieved on account of want of work had increased one hundred and thirty-three per cent. over the previous year's figures. The total body of pauperism, as compared with the total on the same date of the previous year had increased by 3.4 per cent. The new recruits numbered thirty-seven thousand one hundred and seventy-seven. The highest increase was in Durham, 7.1 per cent. One in every thirty-two persons in London is a pauper. It is all due to free trade, cry the Unionists, but Dennis Hathnaught, M. P., representing the Labour party, knows better.

Great attention is now being given in England to the question of the physical deterioration of the English people. This tendency toward degeneracy was brought out very strikingly at the time of the Boer War, when England needed recruits. It has since been reduced to a systematic study. In a medical examination of forty thousand children in various parts of England, thirteen per cent. were found to be suffering from defective vision, one per cent. from heart disease, one per cent. from lung trouble, two per cent. from bodily deformity.

Sir Francis Galton, England's leading authority on the subject of eugenics, held that the bulk of the community was deteriorating, judging from inquiries into the teeth, hearing, eyesight, and malformation of children in board schools and from the apparently continuous increase of insanity and feeble-mindedness. He declared that the popularity of athletics proved little, for it is one thing to acclaim successful athletes, which any mob of weaklings can do, as at a cricket match. It is another thing to be an athlete one's self.

Other features of recent progressive British legislation are measures for a larger income tax and an increase in the taxation of liquors and tobacco; old-age pensions, and compulsory workingmen's insurance. The liquor and tobacco taxes were used by the Conservatives in a telling way with the Hathnaughts. The tax on whiskey was especially odious in Ireland and Scotland, large distilling countries, but bore lighter on England, where there is little distilling, but much brewing of beer. However, Ireland and Scotland, and also Wales, support the Liberals, because of benefits that are expected to come to them in other ways.

In the days of Elizabeth, according to Hume, the House of Commons first ventured to assert its rights as a legislative body, particularly in regard to financial bills. In our day—since 1910, in fact— the House of Lords has been stripped of its power of veto, and can no longer hold back the progress of the country by playing the dog in the manger. Dennis Hathnaught, M. P., is young in legislation, but he is old in memory, and it is written in the Stars that the days of the Lords are numbered, and that their castles are to be dismantled.

CHAPTER XVI.

PATRICK HATHNAUGHT, HOME RULER.

Priestcraft and Parsonolatry have divided Irish Hathnaughts into two hostile camps—Catholics who regard themselves as Irish, and Protestants who are largely anti-Irish and indifferent to the national aspirations. If left to themselves, the Hathnaughts would undoubtedly live in amity and peace, but the curse of dissension and the almost unexampled power of the Catholic and Protestant clergy over their flocks perpetuate a hatred that retards the national prosperity and presents the example of a quick-witted, intelligent race that might be among the world's leaders, retaining an almost mediæval development.

So great is the insistence that education shall be sectarian, that several of the so-called Queen's colleges which are avowedly non-sectarian, have but few students. If a child is a Catholic, the priests demand that he shall be turned over to them; the Episcopal or Church of Ireland clergy are equally zealous that they lose none of their own, and the Presbyterians are no less determined

159

that Presbyterian born Irishmen shall follow in the footsteps of Calvin and Knox. So-called "godless schools" where these children would be taught together, might prove the salvation of the country, but in order to get to Heaven, each by his own route, they have turned the country into a Hell.

It is religion that divides the Irish and not race, for the so-called Scotch-Irish are of blood kindred to that of the native Irish. I might cite a score of authorities to show that Scotia or Scotland was an ancient name of Ireland and that the Scots of to-day are descendants of Irish tribes that centuries ago crossed to North Britain.

In coming to Ireland at the time of the plantation of Ulster under James the first, the Scotch were simply returning to the fatherland. General Stewart of Garth in his famous "Sketches of the Highlanders" declares he often acted as interpreter for Gaelic speaking Irish soldiers, finding their language to differ but little from that of the Highland Scotch. Even the Scotch Lowlander, who now considers himself quite English, spoke Gaelic until the time of Malcolm III (1056) when the king, having married an English princess, introduced English speech, customs, and immigrants into the country. Before the Reformation the native Irish and the new settlers always amalgamated just as Celt, Saxon, Dane and Norman united to form the English race of to-day, but since that great spiritual upheaval, the Irish have divided according to religion. If you are Catholic you are Irish, if not Catholic you get an alibi.

Thus we see S. S. McClure in his "Autobiography" labouring to prove in his first chapter, that although born in Ireland he is a native of Scotland, a notable exception to the rule of Sir Boyle Roche that it is impossible to be in two places at once unless you are a bird. One cannot help thinking that such persons imagine that at the time of the Creation the making of Ireland was let out to a subcontractor who wore a funny little hat, smoked a short clay pipe, and carried his materials in a hod, while gentle zephyrs from the newly made Lakes of Killarney blew through his Galways.

In one of the ablest studies of the Irish question that has ever been made, the preface to "John Bull's Other Island," George Bernard Shaw truthfully contends that it is not the complacent, priest-ridden Catholic who is the typical Irishman and rebel, but the Protestant of the class represented by himself. Joseph McCabe, an "Anglo-Saxon" with a name as Gaelic as Murphy, in his book on Shaw, pooh-poohs the great jester's claim to be Irish and labours to prove that the Irish do not amount to much anyhow. Another McCabe—James D.—reflects the same spirit in a book called "Great Fortunes," when he describes Robert Bonner as "merely a Scotchman born in Ireland." There is paradox for you with the vengeance of the bigot.

An attempt has even been made to show a distinction between Scotch and Irish by claiming that Mac is a Scottish form and Mc an Irish one having no connection with Mac, when the truth is that Mc is only an abbreviation of Mac which means son.

Ireland is the only country in the world that has been systematically deprived of its right to claim its sons and daughters, the minute they engage in any work or art other than carrying the hod or scrubbing floors. In a book called "Race or Mongrel," which is based on the argument that races deteriorate when they practice promiscuity and mix their blood with that of alien people, the author, Alfred Schultz, whose name would probably lead him to be interned in England as a German if he happened to be there during the great war, declares that the English are a race of one blood, the Saxons, Danes and Normans being merely branches of the same great people. He entirely ignores the great Celtic element in the English blood which scholars have recognized and studied since the time Matthew Arnold in his "Celtic Literature," drew attention to the subject. Schultz in dealing with Ireland, ignores the common Gaelic heritage of Ireland and Scotland, and calmly writes down the North Irish as a separate race although if he had the philosophical insight of a sparrow he would have seen that the race difference is almost wholly due to religion and the traditions of religion.

Michael J. F. McCarthy in books called "Priests and People of Ireland," "Rome in Ireland" and similar works has waged, with some encouraging degree of success, a fight against the almost druidical power of the priesthood over the people. He declares that thousands, especially labourers, have fled across the Atlantic and Indian oceans to escape this intolerable thralldom. In Lover's "Rory O'More" there is an amusing account of the hero purchasing a good stout stick for his parish priest to beat his flock with, and this prerogative of power to inflict personal chastisement has not been altogether abandoned by the clergy even in our day.

On the other hand, Orangemen, by perpetuating an asinine idolatry of William III, have been reared in a belief that they are not Irish at all. I remember reading in a book on Ireland written by a Mr. Lynd, an amusing story illustrating this. A friend of Lynd meeting one McCabe, a labourer of some notoriety in his particular town, remarked, "You have a good **Irish** name," whereupon McCabe replied with emphasis, "Irish hell; it is a good Protestant name."

This animosity of Protestant for Catholic and Catholic for Protestant is worked for all it is worth by the great landlord interests. They raise the cry that "Home Rule" means "Rome Rule," but in reality it is the perpetuation of landlord ascendency they are working for, and not religion, for they know full well that there can be no religious persecution under the measure of home rule which the British government aims to establish for the Irish people in a Parliament on Dublin's College Green, at the close of the present world war.

To understand what is meant by Home Rule makes a brief recital of Irish history necessary. From the time of Henry, the second, who came to Ireland under power of a "bull" issued in 1154 by Pope Adrian the fourth, whose family name was Nicholas Brakespere and who was the only Englishman who ever occupied the Papal throne, Ireland has been exploited for the benefit of English rulers and adventurers. There was a time in the history of Ireland when it was no crime for an Englishman to kill an Irishman and when an Irishman could not maintain an action in the courts, no matter how just his cause.

In the time of Elizabeth, according to Froude's "History of England," it was proposed by a company of adventurers to have an "open season" on the Irish and to repopulate the land with English colonists, but the kind suggestion was never acted upon. That Irish life was held cheaply is borne out by Froude, an anti-Irish writer, who tells us that when time hung heavy upon the shoulders of English officers in the "good old days," they had a habit of going out for some "Killings," using the people as game.

The Irish were ordered to adopt the names, customs and language of the invader and after the Reformation, to conform to the established church (Episcopalian). The son of an Irish Catholic upon becoming Protestant could evict his father and assume the ownership of his estates. It was a crime to say the Mass and a capital offense to be a priest. Education, under the old Penal laws was denied to Irish Catholics and it is a matter of historic record that even Daniel O'Connell, the great Irish Liberator, although his father was a member of ancient family and of means, was forced, because of this proscription to learn his first letters from a hedge schoolmaster, a species of instructor unique in the history of education and made necessary by the Penal laws which denied education to Catholics. Gradually the major portion of the land of Ireland was taken from the rightful owners on one pretext or another and parcelled out among English adventurers.

Irish trade was annihilated by British legislative enactments and this brought on conditions that led Dean Swift, one of the greatest leaders of public opinion Ireland ever had, (See Lecky: Leaders of Public Opinion in Ireland) to propose a species of boycott against England at a time when the word boycott was not in use, but the system as a means of achieving an end, well understood. He proposed that Irishmen buy only Irish made goods, and thus bar the English out of Irish markets.

England's difficulty has always been

Ireland's opportunity. In 1782, taking advantage of the American Revolution which was giving England all the trouble she could bear, there was formed an Irish Protestant organization called the Volunteers, ostensibly for the repelling of threatened French invaders, but in reality to bring about the legislative independence of Ireland. These Volunteers under Lord Charlemont forced England to recognize the independence of the Irish Parliament sitting in College Green, Dublin. Of that parliament the greatest orator was Henry Gratton. Curious it was that in this Parliament, representing the people of a country overwhelmingly Catholic, no Catholic could sit.

Presbyterians and other Dissenters had almost as hard a time as the Catholics of Ireland and it is a matter of history that the Irish rebellion of 1798 was largely a Presbyterian rising. The majority of the United Irishmen were Protestants.

Francis McKinley, an ancestor of President McKinley, was one of the Protestant Irish hanged in '98. Green (History of the English People) declares, however, that some of the Catholic rebels used to pounce on and slaughter Protestants just because they happened to be Protestants and that this turning of the national cause into a religious one, alienated the Ulstermen. In 1801 by shameless bribery and the plentiful distribution of titles and privileges, the English government brought about a union of the parliaments of England and Ireland. Then arose the

mighty Daniel O'Connell who had formed
an organization to bring about Catholic
emancipation, a feat he achieved in 1829
when he forced the Duke of Wellington
to consent to a measure of relief as
the alternative of threatened civil war.
O'Connell did not advocate the separation
of Ireland from England as an independent country, believing, according to
Wendell Phillips, that free, Ireland would
be but a petty nation like Portugal and
subject to the bullying of European powers. But he did not believe in permitting
his native land to be exploited by the English. O'Connell had been elected to the
British Parliament before emancipation
had been achieved, but on account of his
religion, had not been permitted to take
his seat. When he did become a member
entitled to speak upon the floor of the
House, he raised his voice in behalf of a
repeal of the Union and the restoration
of Ireland's own parliament.

In 1848 hot headed young Irishmen
under Smith O'Brien started a rebellion
which was an unsuccessful rising.
O'Connell had broken with these young
Irelanders as they were called, and died
of a broken heart.

After O'Connell's death there were no
great, determined efforts to bring about
a repeal of the Union, but in 1872 Mr.
Isaac Butt who had been of counsel for
Smith O'Brien was returned for Limerick
as a Home Ruler and under him the agitation for the repeal of the Union became
a moderate demand for home rule or

self-government in Ireland. Butt was a Protestant but earnestly devoted to his country's welfare. He was finally ousted from the leadership by Charles Stewart Parnell who headed a party demanding a broader measure of self-government than Mr. Butt and his followers had urged.

Mr. Parnell remained leader of the party until 1891 when he was forced into retirement because of his intrigue with the famous Kitty O'Shea, sister of General Evelyn Wood and wife of Captain O'Shea, one of Parnell's followers. Parnell like Butt was a Protestant landholder. Mr. Justin McCarthy, historian and novelist, succeeded to the leadership of a majority of the Irish Nationalist party but a small number remained true to Parnell under the leadership of Mr. John Redmond who eventually succeeded to the leadership of the whole party on the retirement of Mr. McCarthy who was more fitted for the study than for the forum.

Redmond's leadership has been masterly and the consummate ability he has shown in beating down British prejudice has brought home rule within striking distance.

Winston Churchill who braved the wrath of the Orangemen and showed a characteristic contempt for their threats by speaking for home rule in the holy city of the Boyne faction, Belfast, declared the measure would be the means of bringing to an end, an accursed system that made men hate their fellows.

Hopeful signs are not wanting in Ireland that Mr. Churchill's prophecy may come true and that Irish Hathnaughts, unmindful of priest or parson, shall join issues for the rehabilitation of their nation, and work together for the common good. It would be an easy matter for a chemist to prove that there is no difference in the elements that form the waters of the Tiber and the Boyne. All the trouble comes from the attitude of the people that assemble on the banks.

CHAPTER XVII.

SLAVIC HATHNAUGHTS—IVAN AND MICHAEL.

In Russia and Poland the Hathnaughts were subjected until recently to a crushing and grinding serfdom that seemed all but hopeless. Even now that the people are demanding through their Duma some measure of self-government, Ivan, the Russian, and Michael, the Pole, are overwhelmed with grievous taxation that makes their position almost as burdensome as that of the Jews whom they are taught by a vicious State church to persecute and despise. In a history of the common people, it is well worth while to study the conditions under which the Russian and Polish peasants toiled and sweated for an idle, lawless and ignorant nobility.

Rambaud, in his "History of Russia," classifies the Hathnaughts of old Russia under three heads—"The slave or kholop, properly so-called, the mancipium of the Romans, a man taken in war, sold by himself or some one else, or son of a kholop. Second, the peasant inscribed on the lands of a noble, the colonus adscriptius of the Roman Empire, whose person was legally free, but who was to be reduced by means of a more and more rigourous legislation to the condition of krepostnyi or serf of the glebe. Third, the free cultivator who lived like a farmer on the lands of another and had the right to change his master, but who was soon to be mingled with the preceding class."

"It was the inscribed peasant," says Rambaud, "who constituted almost the whole of the rural population. In the ancient provinces the peasant might consider himself as the primitive inhabitant of the soil. He was only made subject to the gentleman in order to secure to the latter an income sufficient for military service; he therefore continued to look on himself as the true proprietor. In these rural masses the primitive features of the Slav organization were preserved in all their vigour. It was the commune or mir, and not the individuals, who possessed the land; it was the commune that was responsible to the Tzar for the tax for the corvee and dues to the lord. This responsibility armed the commune with an enormous power over its members, and this power embodied itself in the starost, assisted by elders.

"In the bosom of the commune the family was not organized less severely, less tyrannically than the mir. The father of the family had over his wife, his sons, married or single, and their wives, an authority almost as absolute as that of the starost over the commune or the Tzar over the Empire. The parental authority became harder and more stern from the contact with serfage and the despotic rule. Ancient barbarism was still intact among these ignorant people; the graceful customs or the savage manners, the poetic or cruel superstitions of the early Slavs, were perpetuated by them. The Russian peasant remained a pagan under his veneer of orthodoxy. His funeral songs seem destitute of all Christian hope. His marriage songs preserve the tradition of the purchase or capture of the bride. The sad lot of the rustic was yet to be aggravated during the three centuries of progress which the upper classes had still to accomplish. In view of the state, as of the proprietor, he tended more and more to become a beast of burden, a productive force to be used and abused at pleasure. . . .

"The starost governed the town and the district depending on it. As the citizens paid the heaviest taxes, they were forbidden to quit the town; they were, as during the last days of the Roman Empire, bound to the city glebe. Alexis Mikhailovitch was afterward to attach the pain of death to this prohibition. To assess the impost, the starost convoked at once both the deputies of the town and those of the rural communities. The impost of the tagla was paid by the town collectively in proportion to the number of fires, and all the people were collectively responsible for each other to the State.

"In the burgess class may be counted the merchants, whose Russian name of gosti (guests or strangers) shows how far commerce still was from being acclimatized in this land and under this régime. Muscovy produced in abundance leather from oxen, furs from the blue and black fox, the zibeline, the beaver, and the ermine; wax, honey, hemp, tallow, oil from the seal, and dried fish. From China, Bokhara, and Persia, she received silks, tea and spices. The Russian people are naturally intelligent and industrious, but still commerce languished.

"Fletcher, the Englishman, has assigned as the reason for this decay the insecurity created by anarchy and despotism. The moujik did not care either to save or to lay by. He pretended to be poor and miserable to escape the exactions of the prince and the plunder of his agents. If he had money he buried it, as one in fear of an invasion.

" 'Often,' says the English writer, 'you will see them trembling with fear, lest a boyard should know what they have to sell. I have seen them at times when they had spread out their wares so that you might make a better choice, look all around them, as if they feared an enemy would surprise them and lay hands on them. If I asked them the cause, they would say to me "I was afraid there might be a noble or one of the sons of the boyards here; they would take away my merchandise by force" ' . . . The citizen, like the inhabitant of the French towns of the fourteenth century, was only a sort of villein; he wore the costume of a peasant and lived almost like him. The merchants were really what they were called by Ivan, the Terrible—the moujiks of commerce."

Two other long-established institutions —domestic slavery and the seclusion of women—have had a marked effect upon the social and industrial life of Russia.

"Besides the peasants more or less attached to the glebe," says Rambaud, "all Russian proprietors kept in their castles, or in their town houses at Moscow, a multitude of servants like those who encumbered the senators' palaces in imperial Rome. A great lord always gathered round him many hundreds of these dvorovie, both men and women bought or born in the house, whom he never paid, whom he fed badly and who served him badly in return, but whose numbers served to give an idea of the wealth of their master.

"The cortège of a noble on his way to the Kremlin may be compared to that of a Japanese daimio. A long file of sledges or chariots, a hundred horses, outriders who made the people stand back by blows with their whips; a crowd of armed men who escorted the noble; and behind a host of dvorovie, often with naked feet beneath their magnificent liveries, filled with their stir and noise the streets of Bielyi-gorod. These domestic slaves were subjected, without distinction of sex, to the most severe discipline, and were forced to submit to all the cruel or voluptuous caprices of their masters, and, like the slaves of antiquity, were exposed to the most frightful chastisements. Whilst the registered colon was attached to the land, the kholopy could be sold, either by heads or by families, without compunction. Wives were separated from their husbands, and children from their parents."

The serf system may be studied from the interesting point of view of fiction from Gogol's "Dead Souls" and Turgenief's short story of "Mumu." It is small wonder that long before Alexander II emancipated the Hathnaughts, March 3, 1861, there had been loud calls for amelioration.

Rambaud describes that other barbarous and oriental system of the Russians—the seclusion of women. Woman was little better off than a slave. A Russian proverb says, "I love thee like my soul and I dust thee like my jacket." She had as little part in the life of her husband until a comparatively modern time—and then only under the French influence—as an ancient Greek woman did. It is related by Rambaud on the authority of Herberstein that a Russian woman, having married a foreigner, did not believe herself loved, as he never beat her. She was in disgrace with the other women who got their chastisement regularly. So widespread was this submission and so thoroughly had the rotten and superstitious Russian Church inculcated it as a duty upon them, that even robust women would willingly submit to be whipped by a feeble husband.

Russian Hathnaughts are robbed and impoverished by the religious and monastic institutions in an even greater degree than are the Spanish people. Shortly after the legal murder of Ferrer, the great educator in Spain, there was an agitation for the suppression of the religious houses. It was shown that these institutions sheltered sixty thousand men and women subject to vows as monks and nuns, who were engaged in productive industries in competition with paid labour and highly taxed manufacturers, but with the advantage to the monasteries of having no taxes to pay or wage scales to meet.

Russia is even more monk and priest-ridden than Spain. In Voltaire's "Charles XII" he describes the Russia of the days before Peter the Great, when the head of the Russian Church possessed power of life and death over all Russians and even the Tzar acknowledged his superior authority by holding the bridle of the horse when the visible head of the church on earth was on parade. Peter changed all that, but the church has never lost its hold upon the people and has been largely instrumental in repressing liberty and persecuting the great writers that have dared to give the living force of words to the national aspirations. The church, too, has always been back of the pogroms. During the massacre of the Jews at Kishineff, the bishop of that place, according to Michael Davitt in "Within the Pale," went about blessing the murderers.

Some notion of the enormous wealth uselessly amassed by the Russian Church in a country subject to periodical distress and famine may be gathered from the following news letter from St. Petersburg, printed in the New York Sun, Sunday, August 31st, 1913:

"The hoarded wealth of the Russian monasteries and convents is certainly immense, although it may not reach the fabulous aggregate of $4,000,000,000, at which popular belief persists in estimating the gold and jewels which the eight hundred and seventy-three recognized religious establishments in the empire have amassed in the course of centuries.

"The Duma when considering this year's budget of the Holy Synod insisted on an inquiry being made into the resources of the religious associations. The results were surprising, for according to official reports the private movable property of all these institutions only amounted to $30,657,500. Their total annual income was placed at $10,000,000 and their expenditure at $9,000,000, $3,-500,000 of which was put down as the cost of maintenance of the archbishops and the monastic fraternities. The value of the land owned by monasteries and convents was estimated at $104,500,000.

"It is hardly necessary to say that no one believes these figures to be anywhere near the truth. It is pointed out that a great number of richly bejeweled saints' images which are well known to the public are worth upward of $500,000 each. Common report places the wealth of the famous Troitzka monastery at $325,000,000, and its possessions in diamonds alone are estimated at $12,500,000."

In Poland we find similar conditions. Campbell in his "Pleasures of Hope" says that "freedom shrieked as Kosciusko fell," but by all accounts the Polish Hathnaught did not lose much when his country was partitioned by Prussia, Russia, and Austria.

In the collected "Political Writings" of Richard Cobden, article "Poland," we read "that, down to the partition of their territory, about nineteen out of every twenty of the inhabitants were slaves, possessing no rights, civil or political— that about one in every twenty was a nobleman—and this body of nobles formed the very worst aristocracy of ancient or modern times; putting up and pulling down their kings at pleasure; passing selfish laws which gave them the power of life and death over their serfs, whom they sold and bought like horses or dogs; usurping, to each of themselves, the privileges of a petty sovereign, and denying to all besides the meanest rights

of human beings; and scorning all pursuits as degrading, except that of the
sword, they engaged in incessant wars
with neighbouring states, or they plunged
their own country into all the horrors
of anarchy, for the purpose of giving
employment to themselves and their dependents."

Cobden continues: "The mass of the
people were serfs, who had no legal protection and no political rights, who enjoyed no power over property of any
kind, and who possessed less security of
life and limb than has been lately extended to the cattle of this island by the
act of Parliament against cruelty to
animals."

Kosciusko fought under Washington
for American independence. It is to be
hoped that in his attempt to reëstablish
the Polish nation he was actuated by a
desire to make his people free in every
sense of the word, in which event it
may be that Campbell was not indulging in poetic license when he said that
"freedom shrieked as Kosciusko fell."

CHAPTER XVIII.

BROTHER JONATHAN AND UNCLE SAM.

Here and there in the homes of those fond of the antique one sees the old spinning wheel, mute evidence of the primitive domestic beginnings of American industry. Now the smokestack is seen in every hamlet in the land and the American manufacturer, a lineal descendant of the house of Hathnaught, is rapidly distancing competitors even in England and Germany.

Brother Jonathan Hathnaught, when he began laying his humble foundation of American industry, was beset with all the vexations incident to the theocracy of Colonial New England when the minister was even more powerful than the governor.

"According to the custom established in Massachusetts," says Richard Hildreth (History of the United States), the Church and State were most intimately blended. The Magistrates and General Court, aided by the advice of the elders, claimed and exercised a supreme control in spiritual as well as temporal matters; while even in matters purely temporal

180

the elders were consulted on all important questions. . . . Besides the Sunday service, protracted to a great length there were frequent lectures on week days, an excess of devotion unreasonable in an infant colony, and threatening the interruption of necessary labour." Hildreth might have added that this "excess of devotion" did not prevent occasional scandal as shown by Hawthorne's "Scarlet Letter" in the relations of Hester Prynne and the young minister, Arthur Dimmesdale.

In addition to religious distinctions, Hildreth says, there were others of a temporal character "transferred from that system of semi-feudal English Society in which the Colonists had been born and bred."

"A discrimination," he goes on to say, "between gentlemen and those of inferior condition was carefully kept up. Only gentlemen were entitled to the prefix of 'Mr.'; their number was quite small, and deprivation of the right to be so addressed was inflicted as a punishment. Good man or good woman, by contraction 'goody,' was the address of inferior persons. . . . All amusements were proscribed; all gayety seemed to be regarded as a sin." If one slandered the government or churches or wrote home discouraging letters, the punishment called for whipping, cropping of ears, and banishment.

It was in this great state monastery of Puritanism where the joyous side of nature and even the natural affections were suppressed, and the conventions that breed deceit, hypocrisy, and oppression were fostered, that Jonathan Hathnaught in the breathing spells between prayer meetings and week-day devotions founded American industrial life.

American industrial supremacy is due not only to the enterprise of Jonathan, but to an unexampled mechanical genius and the development of inventions. Richard Cobden, in an article on "America," in his "Political Writings," bears witness to this.

"The Americans," he says, "possess a quicker mechanical genius than even ourselves (such, again, was the case with our ancestors in comparison with the Dutch), as witness their patents, and the improvements for which we are indebted to individuals of that country in mechanics—such as spinning, engraving, etc. We gave additional speed to our ships by improving upon the naval architecture of the Dutch; and the similitude again applies to the superiority which, in comparison with the British models, the Americans have, for all the purposes of activity and economy, imparted to their vessels."

American industry has been greatly developed by improving the means of transportation, and Cobden contrasts the enthusiasm with which the Americans have established railroads with the indifferent if not hostile attitude of the parliament of his own country.

"The London and Birmingham Company," says Cobden, "after spending upwards of forty thousand pounds in attempting to obtain for its undertaking the sanction of the Legislature, was unsuccessful in the House of Lords."

Cobden gives the following extract from the evidence taken before the committee of those titled boobies:

"Do you know the name of Lady Hastings' place? How near to it does your line go? Taking the look out of the principal rooms of the house, does it run in front of the principal rooms? How far from the house is the point where it becomes visible? That would be a quarter of a mile? Could the engines be heard in the house at that distance? Is there any cutting or embankment there? Is it in sight of the house? Looking to the country is it not possible that the line could be taken at a greater distance from the residence of Lady Hastings?"

Think of it, because an idle, useless, and aimless woman of title might have her slumbers disturbed by the toot of a passing train, rapid transit had to be delayed in England. It is small wonder that patient old John Bull is at last awakening to the necessity of abolishing this house of titled ninnies which has an hereditary right to hold back the nation's progress.

Even in Colonial days, American enterprise had excited the jealousy of the British and the obnoxious stamp act and other exactions led to the American Revolution, which was basically an economic insurrection, notwithstanding the flapdoodle utterances of Fourth of July orators. Within fifty years after this event, American industries had grown to such an extent as to bear comparison with those of England.

In the "American Almanack" for 1835, as quoted by Cobden, we find that the exports from the United States for the year ending Sept. 25, 1833, amounted to $90,140,000, about twenty millions sterling of English money. The British exports for the same period were 47,000,000 pounds, of which 36,000,000 were of home commodities or manufactures, whilst the remaining 11,000,000 consisted of foreign and colonial produce.

"Now," says Cobden, "in order to institute a fair comparison between the respective trades of the two countries, it will be necessary to bear in mind that at the above period, the population of America was about 14,000,000, whilst that of the British empire may be reckoned to have been 25,500,000." Cobden adds that if we note that 2,000,000 of the American population were negroes, the commerce was decidedly in favor of the United States. Manufactures that had an early and rapid development were shipbuilding, the boot and shoe, paper, cordage, nails, and furniture industries. The first growth of these was in New England, and much of it domestic manufacture, unconnected with factory labour, Cobden observes. Indeed, we may remark it was a familiar sight less than thirty years ago, before boot and shoe making machinery revolutionized the business, to find Hathnaughts, fathers and sons, in their own homes or in small bandbox-like workshops busy making footwear.

Cobden's observations are all the more remarkable when one recalls that in 1807, twenty-eight years before, the "embargo" had paralyzed trade. "The sound of the caulking hammer," says John Bach McMaster, in his "History of the People of the United States," "was no longer heard in the shipyards. The sail-lofts were deserted; the rope-walks were closed; the cartmen had nothing to do. In a twinkling the price of every commodity went down, and the price of every foreign commodity went up. But no wages were earned, no business was done, and money almost ceased to circulate." The government, business men, and workingmen suffered immense losses. Thousands became bankrupt, the newspapers were full of insolvent-debtor notices, and post offices and cross-road posts had advertisements of sheriffs' sales.

"In the cities," says McMaster, "the jails were not large enough to hold the debtors. At New York during 1809, thirteen hundred men were imprisoned for no other crime than being ruined by the embargo.

"A traveller who saw the city in this day of distress assures us that it looked like a town ravaged by pestilence. The counting-houses were shut or advertised to let. The coffee houses were almost empty—the streets along the water front were almost deserted. The ships were dismantled; their decks were cleared, their hatches were battened down. Not a box, not a cask, not a barrel, not a bale was to be seen on the wharves, where the grass had begun to grow luxuriantly. A year later eleven hundred and fifty were confined for debts under twenty-five dollars, and were clothed by the Humane Society." Wages in those days, according to McMaster, averaged about one dollar a day.

Cobden's tribute to the mechanical genius of Americans makes it easy to understand the marvellous growth of American industries. That growth may be best studied by turning to encyclopedic articles on the various items of manufacture—cotton, woollens, shipbuilding, cordage, weaving, spinning, boots and shoes, iron, steel, and the like. Its history has also been made the subject of governmental inquiry, and among special works treating of the subject may be mentioned Wright's "Industrial Evolution of the United States."

Jonathan Hathnaught and his Uncle Samuel hold honourable places in the history of labour. From earliest times we read, men have made shoes in Lynn, and Fall River and Lowell long ago became the great centers of the textile trade. In the International Encyclopedia, under the head "Manufactures" we find that the jealousy of the English long prevented our budding manufacturers from making use of the Hargreaves and Arkwright spinning machinery and threw every possible obstacle in the way of American native industries so English trade might control the market.

President Wilson and his supporters have revised the tariff upon a "revenue only" basis. This brings out prominently the fact that our tariff was originally designed to build up our so-called infant industries. Those "infants," tariff reformers say, have been nourished so well upon the tariff milk that they have become giants—trusts, and to some extent agencies for the restraint of trade.

Just how a trust is called into being may be studied in Ida Tarbell's "History of the Standard Oil Company." This company was the first great trust, and continues to be the most powerful one. It is conducted with a masterful grasp of an opportunity that pales the power and achievements of Napoleon.

Socialists of the evolutionary school welcome the trusts which have now invaded all industries, and regard these great corporations as a step in the direction of the ultimate state control of the means of production, distribution, transportation, and communication.

Trusts have been made the subject of governmental investigation largely because of charges of unfair discrimination in their favour by railroads granting rebates, and in May, 1913, a Congressional Committee conducted an inquiry into the workings of the Steel Trust.

Various attempts to dissolve trusts have been made, but with little apparent success. By the very intricacies of their organization they appear to be Protean in their nature and disappear through the exit marked "Dissolution," only to reappear at the entrance marked "Resolved into our original companies." But these companies stick together like Corsican brothers, and the dissolution is apparently hardly more than a name.

It is this concentration of wealth in the hands of a few and the irresponsibility of these few to the people at large that has led to the agitation for the state regulation of trusts, and to outbursts challenging the claim that inheritance is a natural right, and contending that it is a legitimate province of government to turn great fortunes back to the state by legislation. In other words, there is a growing disposition to make wealth assume a definite responsibility and not be governed as in the old days by the whim of the possessor. It is a modern version of the old cry of the utilitarian Bentham, "The greatest good of the greatest number."

George Frisbie Hoar, long a Senator from Massachusetts, in an address before the Chickatawbut Club of Boston, shortly before his death, instanced the following as evils of the trusts:

(1) Destruction of competition.
(2) The management of industries by absentee capital.
(3) Destruction of local public spirit.

(4) Fraudulent capitalization.

(5) Secrecy.

(6) Management for the private benefit of the officers.

(7) The power to corrupt elections, and in some cases to corrupt the courts.

(8) Indifference to public sentiment.

There are three tariff schools in the United States: Protectionists who believe in a high tariff, those who believe in a tariff for revenue only, and free traders. In public life there are few who have dared openly to advocate free trade. Politically therefore we hear of protectionists and tariff reformers who believe in a tariff for revenue only.

Taxes are levied for the support of city, county, state and national government and, according to tariff reformers, should be exacted only to defray the actual expenses of government. Internal revenue is obtained by taxing whiskey, beer, and tobacco. Tariff taxes and duties are collected at "ports of entry." Millions accrue annually to government through tariff taxes, and it is the contention of low tariff advocates that this contracts the volume of the currency and leads to panics. Protection, they declare, keeps up the prices on goods, fosters trusts and corners, and makes paupers on the one hand and millionaires on the other.

Laws of supply and demand regulate the prices of goods and establish the standard of wages. Scarcity of a thing enhances its price; abundance of a thing lowers its price. This holds true also of labour. As Henry George used to say, when two men seek one job, wages are low; when two jobs seek one man, wages are high. If, as protectionists assert, tariff reduction would open American markets to English goods, English wages would increase. Density of population, too, has a great effect on labour.

Opponents of the protective system charge that protection killed American foreign commerce by fettering it with its system. It is held that liberty of exchange, or free trade, is a natural right and that tariff walls interfere with this right and discourage commercial enterprise. Labour creates wealth; restricting trade contracts labour's opportunities and reduces wages, according to economists that favour tariff reduction or its abolition.

It is a noteworthy fact in the history of economic development in the United States that American industries have taken an immense jump forward as the result of the emancipation of the black man —Sambo Hathnaught.

Professor Cairnes, in his work "The Slave Power," finds three fundamental defects in slave labour—it is compulsory and therefore not given willingly; it is unskilful; it is lacking in versatility. It therefore follows that slave labour is only advantageous when concentrated and slaves pursue unskilled vocations.

In his "Democracy in America," De Tocqueville, speaking of the introduction

of the negro slave into the American
Colonies, says: "Slavery, as we shall afterwards show, dishonours labour; it intro-
duces idleness into society, and with idleness ignorance and pride, luxury and distress.   It enervates the powers of the
mind, and benumbs the activity of man.
The influence of slavery, united to the
English character, explains the manners
and social condition of the Southern
States. . . .

"It is not for the good of the negroes,
but for that of the whites, that measures
are taken to abolish slavery in the United
States.   The first negroes were imported
into Virginia about the year 1621.   In
America therefore, as well as on the rest
of the globe, slavery originated in the
South.   Thence it spread from one settle-
ment to another;   but the number of
slaves diminished toward the Northern
States, and the negro population was always very limited in New England.

"A century had scarcely elapsed since
the foundation of the Colonies when the
attention of the planters was struck by
 the extraordinary fact that the Provinces
which were comparatively destitute of
slaves increased in population, in wealth
and in prosperity more rapidly than those
which contained the greatest number of
negroes.   In the former, however, the inhabitants were obliged to cultivate the
soil themselves or by hired labourers; in
the latter they were furnished with hands
for which they paid no wages; yet, although labour and expense were on the

one side, and ease with economy on the other, the former were in possession of the most advantageous system. The consequence seemed to be the more difficult to explain, since the settlers, who all belonged to the same European race, had the same habits, the same civilization, the same laws, and their shades of difference were extremely slight."

Slavery, however, created differences for the Southerner, De Tocqueville says, acquiring through his possession of slaves the idea that he is born to command and who expects to be obeyed without resistance, becomes supercilious, hasty, "irascible, violent and ardent in his desires, impatient of obstacles, but easily discouraged if he cannot succeed upon his first attempt."

The Northerner, on the other hand, having no slaves or even servants about him in childhood, grows self-reliant and learns to supply his own wants.

Since the emancipation of the slaves as a result of the civil war, the old South has disappeared, and a new industrial South is making for prosperity and building up a race of self-reliant and earnest men. The old Southerner, whom Mark Twain declares in his "Life on the Mississippi" built up his ideas of life and chivalry on the basis of Sir Walter Scott's Waverley Novels, again to quote words of the glorious Mark used in another connection, "is a thing of the dead and pathetic past."

CHAPTER XIX.

DENNIS SETTING HIS HOUSE IN ORDER.

. . . . . .

Dennis Hathnaught is showing unmistakable signs of determination to set up governmental housekeeping for himself. In ancient days and throughout the Middle Ages, he was subject to kicks and cuffs and lashings, with no reward for his labour. Little by little all that has been changed. Slavery gradually merged into serfdom and serfdom into paid labour. As time went on, Dennis exhibited greater and greater interest in government, and slowly grew into an enfranchised citizen with a humble, but ever-increasing right to a voice in affairs.

This development of the Hathnaughts from slavery to economic importance in government had its birth in Suggestion. Master minds in their ranks by insinuation, innuendo, or open preaching as in the case of Wamba to Gurth, awakened the dumbwits among the Hathnaughts. Conversation and stories of returning soldiers, itinerant tinkers and peddlers, runaway slaves and serfs, concerning movements taking place elsewhere, all had an effect through Suggestion upon the enslaved masses and led them, in imitation of their fellows, to revolt and to demand amelioration of conditions and a share in the harvests they reaped. Since the invention of printing the work of awakening the people has been marvellously accelerated.

Every mental operation is in the nature of Suggestion. In works on psychology you will read of consciousness, sub-consciousness, somnambulism, hypnotism, perception, understanding, memory, habit, imagination, judgment, conception, sensations, sight, touch, feelings, scent, hearing, irritability, desires, admiration, contempt, compassion, emotions, attention, association of ideas, volition, motives, reason, relativity of knowledge, resemblances, right and wrong, sagacity (especially in animals), sympathy, thought, truth, vision—all subject to Suggestion growing out of the mysterious processes of the mind whereby one fact in association with another or by contrast with it, brings forth the Suggestion that later becomes a new incentive to action and further progress. Even speech originated in suggestion if the onomatopoeic theory is correct—that language owes its origin to man's attempt in the beginning to adapt words to sounds. Hiss, cackle, caw, buzz, are instances of sound imitation.

Like everything else, government is the result of Evolution and Suggestion. No man or group of men has yet been able to frame a Constitution or Code of Laws that may become the fixed, unalterable source of governmental powers for all time. Even our own Constitution that we regard as reverently as the Carthaginians did the sacred garment of Tanit, does not always work out the problem as the Fathers intended it should.

Human improvement is born of Suggestion growing out of Precedent, and Liberty is the result of many concessions often wrung painfully from the ruling classes. Were we to reëstablish suddenly the slavery of Greece and Rome, every man, woman, and child would see the injustice and iniquity of it, for we now possess the historic sense and the historic background to judge it by. But many fine men and women of antiquity, with nothing different to look backward to, approved of slavery and saw no injustice in an idle group reaping the full benefit of the labour of an active and enslaved class.

The best of all Constitutions is the British Constitution for it has the advantage of not being a set and written document and may thus grow by accessions. It is in reality nothing but the digested spirit of laws safeguarding human rights, such as the Magna Charta, the immortal habeas corpus act which guarantees a person against unjust seizure and incarceration; right of trial by jury in open court, and the right to challenge men called to the panel; religious freedom and toleration; right of assembly and petition; the tendency toward an

equitable adjustment of taxation; gradual abolition of exemptions and privileges enjoyed by the nobility and clergy;
procedure under due process of law so
that citizens may not fear imprisonment
or confinement in madhouses without
form of trial or the procuring of a writ
or warrant.

Dennis Hathnaught is working through
Trades-Unions, Socialism, and Syndicalism, as well as through the old political
parties, which he is beginning to suspect,
are simply nest-builders for political
cuckoos. If any one ever adapts Othello
to the labour question, Dennis as Othello will have the professional politician
for his Iago or false friend.

In a book purposely kept within short
compass, it would be impossible to discuss exhaustively the phases of
economic evolution, and in our account
here of Trade-Unionism, Socialism, and
Syndicalism, we shall touch only upon
the surface, giving the untrained reader
just enough to enable him to go intelligently into a deeper study of the movements.

Trades-Unionism may be said to date
from the first conference of slaves, impatient to shed their chains. In Eugene
Sue's curious work, "The Mysteries of
the People; or History of a Proletarian
Family Across the Ages," we find reference to the "Sons of the Mistletoe," an
organization of Gallic Hathnaughts in
Ancient Rome which met in a cave,
members often dragging their heavy

chains to the meeting place. Their aim
was to throw off the yoke of their masters, but in reality it was an economic
movement and may be cited as an early
example of the trades-union.

Again, the agrarian agitation on the
part of the plebeian population of Rome
itself, led to the organization of guilds
that had in them the germ of trades
unionism and socialism.

In the Middle Ages the Guilds were organizations of tradesmen, but with this
difference—they included masters as well
as workmen. For the student curious to
trace the history of these now powerful
organizations, we may refer to Thorold
Rogers' "Six Centuries of Work and
Wages," Gibbins' "Economic History of
England," Webbs' "History of Trades
Unionism," Brentano's "Guilds and
Trades Unions," and Fawcett's "Political
Economy." Professor Fawcett was a
member of the "Social Science Committee on Trade Societies," which made an
exhaustive report on the general subject
of workmen's organizations which is still
a standard authority. This report was
published in England in 1860.

Objects of unions in the main are to
regulate the hours of labour and to set
the standard of wages. The unions from
the very beginning of their history have
contended for the right to control the apprentice system, which in the old days
constituted a kind of serfdom in which
the apprentice was bound by strict articles of indenture to serve his master

while learning a trade. Nowadays, an apprentice may abandon his work at will, but in earlier times he was liable to the law. The idea of the unions in controlling the apprentice system was to keep trades from becoming overcrowded, and so well was this done by the unions that in the city of Lynn, Mass., the backbone of the shoemakers' unions and their monopoly of the labour supply was not broken until the importation of cheap Italian and Armenian labour led the manufacturers to the breaking in of green hands when their skilled workmen were on strike.

With the rise of an independent and class-conscious working class in England, after the "Black Death," when labour was exceedingly scarce, the Hathnaughts asserted a right to have a word in the matter of wages and hours of labour.

Thorold Rogers, in his "Six Centuries of Work and Wages," calls the time from the peasants' rebellion in 1381 to the reign of Henry VIII, "the golden age of the English Labourer," for his fight for recognition led to better wages, shorter hours, and more certainty of employment. This, too, despite the fact that the government, leagued with the great land owners, endeavoured to stay the progress of labour toward independence and self-regulation.

As we understand the trades union of today, it may be said to have been in existence for four hundred years approximately, for in 1548, in the reign of Edward VI, as shown by the statutes of England, a law was aimed against workmen, who had combined and taken an oath to do only certain kinds of work and to regulate the method of doing it, the hours and the compensation. There is abundant evidence by Froude, Macaulay, and other historians that the government for centuries tried to control labour arbitrarily, and it was not until 1824 that it became legal for workmen through organization to set a value upon their own labour and to have a say about hours and other conditions.

The Chartist movement in England was the outgrowth of a growing sense of independence on the part of labour and its demand for political rights. Chartism has a literature of its own besides being incorporated in every history of the early years of Queen Victoria's reign. It had its origin in a state of low wages accompanied by a high cost of living. The agitation raged for ten years and occasioned great public excitement. Oddly enough, one of the most famous leaders of this uprise of the English proletariat was one Feargus O'Connor, a celebrated mob orator who claimed descent from Brian Boru. The agitation which resulted in monster petitions to parliament, occasioned great alarm in conservative England, and disturbances led to bloodshed.

Demands of the Chartists as we view such matters today, were very moderate. They were six in number—first, annual

Parliaments; second, Universal Suffrage; third, Vote by ballot; fourth, Equal Electoral Districts; fifth, Abolition of Property Qualifications for members of Parliament; sixth, Payment of members of Parliament.

Most of these demands are now the law of the land and labour has made such headway politically that we have the spectacle of sixty labour members sitting in the British Parliament, and constituting the backbone of radical legislation.

The initiative, the referendum, the recall, employers' liability legislation, compulsory insurance, old-age pensions, woman suffrage, commission government, and like legislation are all manifestations of the presence of Dennis Hathnaught in Congress, Parliament, Reichstag, and Duma.

Socialism also is ancient of days. Lassalle calls Heraclitus, a pre-Socratic Greek philosopher (535-475 B. C.), the father of Socialism. Many of the early insurrections, particularly the risings under Spartacus and Wat Tyler were socialistic in character, but it has been only since the French Revolution that the idea of social equality has assumed a political importance.

Rousseau was a great detached teacher of Socialism. In his "Social Contract" he stirred the nation with his famous sentence, "Man is born free but is everywhere enslaved." In this work he advanced principles that made his book a kind of Bible to the revolutionists and made a sharp attack upon the claim of the landowner and the nobly born to exclusive privilege of wielding political power. The labourer whose toil made it possible for the State to exist, Rousseau maintained, had a right to participate in the business of government.

Henri Alphonse Esquiros, a Frenchman (1812-1876), in his "Evangel of the People," pictures Christ as a socialist teacher in full sympathy with the industrial revolutionary movement. This was published in 1840 and its author's reward was eight months' imprisonment and a fine of five hundred francs. The France of that day wanted no preachers of revolution, least of all economic revolution through the medium of the founder of Christianity.

Karl Marx was the founder of international socialism. His battle cry, "Workingmen of the World, unite," is still the rallying slogan of the social revolution whether that revolution takes the form of trades-unionism, socialism, or syndicalism. His great work, "Capital," displays a wonderful grasp upon the fundamentals of economics and the knowledge he shows of economic literature is enormous and intimate. His work has been translated into many languages and besides epitomes gotten out by socialistic publishers, there is available in English, a good translation edited by Fred Engels.

One of the earliest attempts in the

United States to bring the levelling process to bear upon the classes of society was the Brook Farm experiment in which George Ridley, Nathaniel Hawthorne, Albert Brisbane, Margaret Fuller, and some other of the noted persons of the day took part. Its effort to achieve equality and solve the vexed labour problem failed, but the experiment, besides the usual historical accounts that preserve its memory, is immortalized by Hawthorne in "The Blithedale Romance."

Frederick Spielhagen, in his novel, "Hammer and Anvil" (1869), gives us a study of the warring castes of Germany as affected by the peculiar nature of German institutions. We must choose whether we will be the hammer or the anvil, he says, and tries to point a way out by declaring that it shall not be hammer or anvil, but hammer and anvil, for, he says, everything and every human being is both at once and every moment.

In Germany, where Socialism has had a wonderful expansion, one of the great leaders was August Bebel. In his "Woman under Socialism," he notes the importance of the female sex in the economic evolution of the race, and declares that her emancipation and perfect equality with man is the goal of all social development—a foregone conclusion which no power can alter or set aside. As a step in this direction, the rule of man over man, and capitalist over workman, he declares, must be abolished.

Then, he thinks, will come the Golden Age, for which men have dreamed for centuries, and with the end of class rule, will come the end of the rule of man over woman.

Whatever the motive of titled women in taking up the cause of militancy and demanding the ballot, there is no doubt that the great feminist movement of to-day is an outgrowth of socialistic agitation. Olive Schreiner, in her notable work, "Woman and Labour," calls the feminist movement a sex revolt against parasitism. In her demand that woman shall become a producer and a worker, instead of becoming a doll or a mere population increaser, she takes her place beside the John the Baptists of Progress, who are crying aloud in the wilderness of our modern industrial world.

Those who think women in politics a modern phenomenon would do well to open their Livy and read about the furore caused by C, Oppius proposing a law in Ancient Rome, long before the Christian era, forbidding women the use of golden ornaments. In the debate that followed, the way the women went out into the highways and byways, besieging influential men and agitating for the repeal of the law, would put cheer into Mrs. Pankhurst's soul during a hunger strike. Every "Jeremiah" who pours out lamentations against "Maria" and her "Votes for Women" militancy, would do well to read these luminous pages of Livy. After all, it may be that militancy

is only atavistic. Our modern suffra-
gettes may be descendants of those old
Roman matrons.

In harmony with this growing feminist spirit is the demand for the single
moral standard for men and for women.
Mrs. Hathnaught is not only demanding
the vote, but she is showing an impatience with the reckless deductions of
sociological scamps and ecclesiastical
windbags who are always holding inquis-
itorial sessions over feminine morals.
There should be some legal penalty to
reach scoundrels who make wholesale
charges, not backed by evidence, that
girls in department stores eke out an additional income through secret prostitu-
tion. Turn around is fair play, and it
would be in line for women to challenge
these critics by inquiring into their own
moral standards which, as frequent
newspaper exposures show, are often
more or less mangy.

There is some truth in the epigram
that mankind may be divided into two
classes—the guilty and the undetected. A
militant branch of the undetected may
be called the Flying Squadron of Virtue.
The mission of this precious corps is to
push little Miss Foundout and her lover,
Mr. Haha You Villain, into the ranks of
the guilty. This done, they sing a pean,
for the triumph of the righteous and the
glory of the good.

Anti-suffragists are fond of dilating on
the home, yet the home as we know it, is
a very modern institution. They go into

ecstacies over the so-called sweet womanhood of yesterday. Yet these poor
souls were hardly more than sex manni-
kins who had their lovers picked out for
them by autocratic fathers and whose ignorance was such that their conversation seldom went beyond the small scan-
dals and the society flapdoodle of the
boudoir. In that charming Scotch Comedy, Moffat's, "Bunty Pulls the Strings,"
there is a fine representation of the old-
fashioned religious home, but for my own
part I would rather spend a week's end
in jail than a Sabbath day with Tammas.

Socialists claim to have suffered im-
mensely from misrepresentation and prejudice. The Papal authorities, they assert, have organized a band of lay Jesuits,
the Knights of Columbus, to fight them
on the ground that socialism is an im-
moral movement that threatens the home
and the sanctity of marriage.

In Germany the movement has been
combated by prosecution and imprisonment, but it has covered the prison walls
like ivy and has spread itself over the
land.

Any cut-and-dried Utopian programme
for the righting of human wrongs is best
fought by reason and frank discussion,
and not by hatred and intolerance. It is
the hardest thing in the world to make
people see things justly and impartially.
The best of us either condemn or condone according to our prejudices or pred-
ilections. We may illustrate our point
by a triangle:

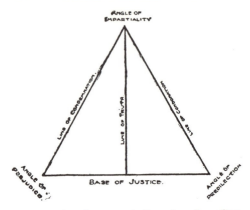

He who has prejudice be he Conservative or Socialist, will always look along the line of condemnation. In like manner the man with predilection will excuse or condone. But he who looks down from the angle of impartiality can see at once the lines of condemnation and condonation as well as the straight line of truth that leads to the Base of Justice.

Socialism aims to establish the coöperative Commonwealth, and its motto is "To each according to his deeds." It would level class distinctions, make the world a great body of producing workmen, and by giving every man the full fruit of his labour, do away with the wage system which socialists term economic slavery. Under this system the State would control the means of production, transportation, and distribution. In the view of the Socialist the workingman is nothing more than a ticket of leave serf.

Now we have to deal with Syndicalism and Sabotage, both French in their origin. Since the great strike in Lawrence and in 1913 with the strike in Paterson, N. J., under the Industrial Workers of the World, we have heard much of Syndicalism. In the last few years, thanks to the ever-growing interest in economics, we have seen many volumes on the subject issue from the press.

Socialism contends that it would emancipate labour by gaining control of the government; Syndicalism would achieve a like result by getting control of industries through the medium of Unions. Socialism finds its weapon in the ballot; the Syndicalist, in the general strike or so-called direct action. Sabotage and boycotting are instruments of the movement supplementary to the general strike.

Discussing the new movement, the New York *Evening Post* quoted one of its leaders as follows:

"Fellow-workers, you want an eight-hour day. Well, take it, and when you come back the next morning, tell the master you were on strike four hours yesterday.

"You want to get possession of the instruments of production? You are in possession already. All you have to do is to declare you own the factory in which you work. If the master protests, lock him out. You say you don't get the full value of your toil? Get it, do only as much work as you are paid for, and go slow the rest of the time. You say the machinery ruins your health? Ruin the machinery for a while. You say you are treated like dirt? Put some dirt into the product." This injury to machinery and product constitutes Sabotage. The word comes from sabot, French for shoe, and originated in a "pleasant" little custom of disgruntled workmen throwing their wooden shoes into machinery and wrecking the finely adjusted mechanism.

Socialism would substitute the State for the individual proprietor; Syndicalism on the other hand aims at a decentralizing effect whereby the whole body of workers in various places, represented on trade councils will control the industries that supply the demands of society without the interference of a central government. In this way trade centres would become communes. Syndicalism does not divide the workers into separate unions. It takes in all workers indiscriminately, and by making the cause of one the concern of all, aims to have the workers strike as one man. The Syndicalist thus regards himself as a true democrat. The old trade unionist with his exclusive trade organization, is looked upon as an aristocrat.

The non-producer or, as the Syndicalists call him, the parasite of society, would, it is asserted, automatically become non-existent. Thus we might see the spectacle of a duke exchanging his

coronet for a hod and the old English
Squire dropping the golf stick for the
shovel.

Important recent works are "Syndical-
ism and Labour," by Sir Arthur Clay;
"Syndicalism and the General Strike," by
Arthur D. Lewis; "American Syndical-
ism—the Industrial Workers of the
World," by John Graham Brooks; "The
New Unionism," by Andre Tridon.

Syndicalism is such a radical advance
over ordinary Socialism that it may result in many conservatives finally becoming Socialists to fight this more advanced and revolutionary development
of economic thought.

But Socialism is far from being the
Ultima Thule of Government. Its greatest weakness is a tendency toward dog-
matism. The revolutionary Socialist hates
the Fabian and the Communist and Syndicalist hate the moderate Socialist. The
form of organization, or tyranny of the
group tends to minimize the object
sought, just as in some religious bodies,
the way you worship seems to count for
more than what you worship and why
you worship. Just as nature is governed
by the power inherent in the atom, so
must all true and lasting progress de-
pend upon the improvement of the individual man—the race unit.

Opponents of Socialism declare that
the weakest point in the movement is
the supposed disinclination of man to
labour. With growing intelligence this
ancient prejudice toward labour is dying

out. Labour is assuming a dignity which makes it a reproach to be an idler and last of all, as Fourier shows, labour may be made attractive. If this could be done, John Stuart Mill says, the principal difficulty of Socialism would be overcome.

Socialism is but a milestone in the progress of Dennis Hathnaught. What is to come after it we know not, for it is not given to man to lift the veil of the future. Keep up your courage and trudge on. Your journey is unending. In Swedenborg, Browning, and others of the thinking tribe, you will find thoughts that combat the idea of finality. Walt Whitman, the poet of Democracy, a man jocund with the zest of living, held to the belief that "it is provided in the essence of things that from any fruition of success, no matter what, shall come forth something to make a greater struggle necessary."

There is no place for the loafer in the scheme of that mysterious thing we call Life. The soul never dies nor does personal identity die. Man cannot escape his Destiny and suicide does not end suffering. What you do Here counts for you There. You must face the issue and here or somewhere, man must do his work. This journey of ours had no beginning and it will never have an end. We pass from the nadir to the zenith only to find that what we thought the zenith is but the nadir of new heights. Courage, and trudge on—up, up, up, ever in pursuit of the Ultimate which beckons to us but never waits.

CHAPTER XX.

DENNIS INQUIRING INTO LAND TITLES.

Rousseau, borrowing a thought from Pascal, declared the first man who enclosed a piece of land the real founder of society. All through history the great struggle has been between those that own land and those that are landless. If you possess nothing it is easy to convince yourself that you should have a share of your neighbour's property. Analyze the arguments of many pseudo socialists who confound their covetousness with conviction, and you will find their basis in the fable of the two Irishmen, one of whom possessed two goats, while the other had none.

One of the most radical proposals to settle the land question is that put forth by Henry George in his "Progress and Poverty"—a system which has become widely known under the familiar economic name of the "Single Tax." Mr. George would abolish all taxes save that on land. By exempting improvements and taxing land to its full value he would do away with speculation in land, and real estate brokers would not find it profitable, he contends, to hold unimproved land as they do at present, waiting to take advantage of new public works or the enterprise of contiguous landowners, to enhance, without expense to themselves, the value of land held for speculation.

Under the present system, if an apartment house faces desirable property—say the home of a wealthy man with its park and gardens—the Hathnaughts in the apartments are likely, according to single taxers, to pay a far higher rental than if the outlook were upon a factory.

The difference between the rent Hathnaught pays and what he would be charged were there a factory fronting him instead of the well-kept home of the millionaire, constitutes, in the view of single taxers, an unearned increment.

In a humorous way the following story from Harper's Magazine illustrates the manner in which the "unearned increment" operates and is sometimes circumvented:

An old coloured woman came into a Washington real-estate office the other day and was recognized as a tenant of a small house that had become much enhanced in value by reason of a new union station in that neighbourhood.

"Look here, auntie, we are going to raise your rent this month," the agent remarked briskly.

"'Deed, an' ah's glad to hear dat, sah," the old woman replied, ducking her head politely. "Mighty glad, fo' sho', case ah des come in hyah terday ter tell yo' all dat ah couldn't raise hit dis month."

In a certain measure Mr. George's system has been introduced into that great experiment station of civilization and laboratory of economics—New Zealand, where it is no longer possible to alienate land. Lloyd George and his followers, in a modified form, are applying the principle to the land question in England.

The physiocrats, a group of French economists of the eighteenth century, held views that were in many particulars like those of Mr. George, especially in regard to what they called the "Impot Unique," which resembled the single tax. It was the contention of the physiocrats that land was the only source of wealth. A surplus was produced through cultivation and nature's free and generous help, and this surplus, the excess of the value of the product over its cost, the physiocrats called the "Produit Net." As land is the great source of wealth there is naturally competition for its use, and this brings the prospective tenant into negotiations with the landlord. In this way the tenant is forced to hand over to the landlord the greater part of the "Produit Net" under the name of rent.

François Quesnay (1694-1774), one of the leading physiocrats, noted three classes—the farmer whose first hand devotion to agriculture produced the "Produit Net"; the landlord who waited until the harvest was garnered and then, without the turn of a hair, collected most of the "Produit Net" in the name of rent; lastly, the manufacturers and their like— the so-called "Sterile Class"—who eventually got what was left.

Quesnay, developing his argument from the conditions, which he held to be self-evident facts, contended that a tax on land, the "impot unique," was the only legitimate form of taxation. It was Quesnay who invented the term "Political Economy," but later thinkers do not agree with his characterization of manufacturers as a "Sterile Class," because they do not produce wealth, but simply alter its shape. The manufacturer adds utility to a thing which had not previously possessed this attribute, and thus they add to human happiness by meeting human wants—a work that can hardly be called sterile.

Adam Smith, author of "The Wealth of Nations," the real founder of the science of Political Economy, pays a high tribute to the worth and value of the labours of the physiocrats. Some approximation also to their theories and the theories of Mr. George will be found in Herbert Spencer's "Social Statics," in which it is held that "equity does not permit property in land." "Supposing," he argues, "the entire habitable globe to be so enclosed, it follows that if the landowners have a valid right to its surface, all who are not landowners have no right at all to its surface. Hence, such can exist on the earth by sufferance

only. They are all trespassers. Save by
the permission of the lords of the soil,
they can have no room for the soles of
their feet. Nay, should the others think
fit to deny them a resting place, these
landless men might equitably be expelled
from the earth altogether."

Spencer, although he changed his views
in later life, very clearly foreshadows
the principle of land nationalization which
Mr. George advances in "Progress and
Poverty" and other economic works.

Since the fall of the feudal system the
leasing of land to tenants has taken various forms. The usual way is a direct
rental, but in Italy and some other countries we find the Metayer system, whereby the landowner takes his pay in a
portion of the produce. In the United
States this is called "taking a farm on
shares." It is fully described by Fawcett and other political economists. In
Ulster, in the North of Ireland, there has
long been a check on the avarice of landlords, called the "tenant right," whereby the Hathnaught may get some return
for his enterprise and may realize on
his good will.

In developing his land theory in "Progress and Poverty," Henry George combats the principles set forth by Malthus
in his "Essay on Population." This work
appeared in 1798 and has been the subject of world-wide controversy. Briefly
Malthus, who foreshadowed the law of
natural selection, held that the human
race possesses the possibility of increas-

ing faster than the supply of subsistence; that while population might double in a quarter of a century, it was unlikely that the means of subsistence would do so.

The Malthusian laws are three in number:

First—Population is limited by means of subsistence.

Second—Population increases when the means of subsistence increase unless interrupted by checks.

Third—These checks which hold population down to the level of subsistence are vice, misery and moral restraint.

Darwin also takes note of the Malthusian propositions and shows the effect of natural selection and the law of the survival of the fittest in modifying the laws of Malthus. Few persons are now alarmed by these propositions which grew out of wrongs and conditions that obtained in the days of Malthus, but which are now happily being corrected by freer trade and other intelligent legislation and a more enlightened view on the part of the population as to man's place in nature.

Men and women are not so prone nowadays to bring into the world children damned from birth to lives of degradation and misery. "Moral restraint" is developing into the new science of eugenics or race selection.

CHAPTER XXI.

DENNIS BECOMES A LITERARY HERO.

While we find incidental references to labour in ancient books, it is only within the last century that Dennis Hathnaught has been considered of sufficient importance to have books written about him as the main theme. Macaulay makes a kind of apology in his "History of England" for his slight attention to the common people, and sets down as the cause the scantiness of the materials of their history.

"Literature during many ages," says Buckle (History of Civilization), "instead of benefiting society, injured it by increasing credulity, and thus stopping the progress of knowledge. Indeed, the aptitude for falsehood became so great that there was nothing men were unwilling to believe. Nothing came amiss to their greedy and credulous ears. Histories of omens, prodigies, apparitions, strange portents, monstrous appearances in the heavens, the wildest and most incoherent absurdities, were repeated from mouth to mouth, and copied from book to book, with as much care as if they were the choicest treasures of human wisdom.

"Instead of telling us those things which alone have any value, instead of giving us information respecting the progress of knowledge, and the way in which mankind has been affected by the diffusion of that knowledge, instead of these things, the vast majority of historians fill their works with the most trifling and miserable details: personal anecdotes of kings and courts; interminable relations of what was said by one minister, and what was thought by another, and, what is worse than all, long accounts of campaigns, battles, sieges, very interesting to those engaged in them, but to us utterly useless, because they neither furnish new truths, nor do they supply the means by which new truths may be discovered.

"This is the real impediment which now stops our advance. It is this want of judgment, and this ignorance of what is most worthy of selection, which deprives us of materials that ought long since to have been accumulated, arranged, and stored up for future use. In other great branches of knowledge, observation has preceded discovery; first the facts have been registered, and then their laws have been found. But in the study of the history of man, the important facts have been neglected, and the unimportant ones preserved."

All this is changing. Green wrote a

history of the English people rather than a history of England. In America J. B. McMaster has done a like service for the "People of the United States." From the press there is pouring out daily books innumerable touching upon labour and the social revolution. The writers sometimes use the poetical form, then again fiction, history, or the form of special treatise. The movement has invaded the stage, and some notable plays have been produced within the last few years, which touch upon the life and struggles of the Hathnaughts.

Publishers' statements—particularly a striking one in the *Atlantic Monthly* by a member of the Macmillan firm—show that there is a lessening demand for old books, and a marvellous increase in the public taste for new fiction. But it is a cheering note of the times to hear that on the other hand there is a great and growing public that calls for solid books on economic questions and even the most conservative of the publishers are now supplying these, many of them revolutionary in their character.

The first mighty blow struck at foolish literature was that of Cervantes in "Don Quixote," which laughed the absurdities of the Age of Chivalry out of existence.

Lord Morley of Blackburn (John Morley), in a study of "Diderot and the Encyclopaedists," points out the power wielded by these precursors of the French Revolution, by combining with the scientific idea the social idea. Old intellectual insurgents like Abelard, Bruno, and Vanini, he says, had felt the iron hand of the church because, with all their philosophy and science, they lacked the social idea. The Encyclopaedists, combining the scientific with the social idea, met the Church on new ground and with a new weapon.

"Its leaders," Morley says, "surveyed the entire field with as much accuracy, and with as wide a range as their instruments allowed; and they scattered over the world a set of ideas which at once entered into energetic rivalry with the ancient scheme of authority. The great symbol of this new comprehensiveness in the insurrection was the Encyclopaedia. . . . Broadly stated, the great moral of it all was this: that human nature is good, that the world is capable of being made a desirable abiding place, and that the evil of the world is the fruit of bad education and bad institutions. This cheerful doctrine now strikes on the ear as a commonplace and a truism. A hundred years ago in France it was a wonderful gospel, and the beginning of a new dispensation. . . . Every social improvement since has been the outcome of that doctrine in one form or another."

No summary of facts bearing upon the house of Hathnaught would be complete without reference to the important part played by the "Encyclopedie." Breathing as it did the broadest humanity and sympathy with the Hathnaughts and human progress; subordinating the church to science and the service of man, it appeared at a time when the people were ripe for revolution. The old order was changing, and the "Encyclopedie" hurried the process of the change. It was projected by men who were impatient of all restraint upon liberty, and its thirty-five volumes were completed between the years 1751 and 1780. Within twenty-five years the spark thus ignited burst into the conflagration known as the French Revolution.

We see the mob element in Katherine Pearson Woods novel, "Metzerott, Shoemaker." This is a modern study of socialism with an American setting in an industrial center called "Micklegard." Karl Metzerott, the hero, will not stick to his last, but concerns himself with the social revolution as he sees it in his community. Free thinker in religion and socialist in political bent, he dreams of a day when America will be a vast co-operative commonwealth. With some others he establishes a co-operative business which meets with success. But there are warnings of an explosion in the discontent of the Hathnaughts, and when the breaking of a dam at the private fish pond of the ruling caste brings on a flood, there is only needed the death of a poor victim to bring out the mob spirit. Metzerott leads the Hathnaughts that are bearing down upon the home of Randolph, the town's wealthiest citizen, to wreak vengeance, when a bullet

ends the life of the shoemaker's son
Louis, and the mob is turned into mourners about the grief-crazed father.

Class jealousy, which makes the Hathnaughts suspicious of any of their number seen fraternizing with the caste above
them, is shown in "The Mutable Many,"
by Robert Barr (1896). The scene is
London, and the theme the social revolution. During a strike, Sartwell, manager of the factory affected, will not
deal with the strikers as a body, but he
does meet Marsten, one of the men, and
as individuals they review the clashing
issues.

Marsten, although he loves Edna Sartwell, the manager's daughter, is loyal
to his class, and the fight continues, with
the result that the strike is lost, and
Marsten finds himself dismissed as workman and lover. He is made secretary of
the union, and tries to win Miss Sartwell, although he has a rival for her
hand in Barney Hope, son of one of the
mill owners. She refuses them both.

There is a second strike at the works
and Marsten has this so well under way
that success is in sight, when Edna Sartwell calls at the union headquarters to
plead with Marsten to let her father win
and thus retain his ascendency at the
works, offering him her hand as a reward. He will not listen to what he
considers a dishonourable proposal, but
the interview has sealed his fate, for the
Hathnaughts jump to the conclusion that
he is betraying them. He is so severely

treated in consequence that he has to undergo attention at a hospital. Sartwell easily defeats Marsten's successor and what might have been a winning fight under the old secretary becomes rout under the new. But Marsten in the end wins the girl.

Some years ago "The Breadwinners," a powerful study of the labour question, attracted wide attention, and there was much speculation concerning the identity of the author. A member of, the old firm of Harper's which published the book, not long ago revealed the author in the person of the late John Hay. In his lifetime Mr. Hay never acknowledged it, despite its wide circulation and frequent intimations that the novel was from his pen.

In "The Breadwinners" is depicted the worst side of the labour question—the rascally, demagogic leader and the easily inflamed mob. Maud Matchin, daughter of a Western carpenter in business for himself, is loved by one of her father's workmen, Sam Sleeny, but she has taken a violent fancy to Alfred Farnham, formerly an army officer, and tells him so.

Maud is fair to look upon, but environment and lack of culture have put the vulgar taint upon her, and, of course, she does not appeal to Farnham, who has brought about the situation by showing an interest in the girl. Farnham really loves the beautiful Alice Belding.

As the story develops, Farnham organizes a volunteer band to protect property during a great strike which breaks out, and in an attack upon his home by the rioters, Sleeny hits him with a hammer. Poor Sleeny if left to himself would not be a bad sort of fellow, but he is under the influence of Offitt, an unscrupulous and dishonest labour leader, and had grown jealous of Farnham, whom he mistakes for a rival.

Maud feels that Farnham should be punished for his treatment of her, and Offitt, with a view to winning her for himself, gets a hammer from Sleeny, and entering Farnham's house, assaults and robs him. Sleeny is arrested for the crime after Offitt has cast suspicion upon him. Offitt tries to induce Maud to fly with him, but she will have none of him, and learning the truth from his admissions, she makes it known. Sleeny would have been cleared of the charge, but before his innocence is established he breaks jail, and meeting Offitt at Maud's house, kills him. Tried for this murder, he is acquitted, as it is held he must have been insane at the time.

Alice Belding and her mother nursed Farnham after Offitt's murderous attack on him, and Alice, who had previously refused him, finds that in reality she cares for him a great deal.

In noticing books dealing with the Hathnaughts we should not overlook those powerful stories in the "Epic of the Wheat," Frank Norris's "The Octopus" and "The Pit." The first deals with wheat in the growing; "The Pit" deals

with the Chicago wheat pit. A third novel
to complete a trilogy was to have been
called "The Wolf," and was to have dealt
with a famine in Europe, but this was
not completed when the author died.
Norris portrays with startling vividness
the manner in which railroads and corporations rob the farmer and control
legislation.

A notable recent novel, "The Inside of
the Cup," by Winston Churchill, is a
worth-while study of social conditions,
especially of the use some unscrupulous
wealthy men make of the church as a
cloak for their hypocrisy.

CHAPTER XXII.

HATHNAUGHT VERSUS HAVE-AND-HOLD.

Romance and tales of chivalry have thrown a glamour about the old nobility, yet in the main the Lords of Have-and-Hold were barbarous, illiterate and uncouth. Their principal occupations were rioting, war, wholesale robbery, oppression of the Hathnaughts, feastings, and tournaments. They seldom bathed and their table manners were often worse than those of a 'longshoreman. Charlemagne with all his authority failed when he tried to introduce schools, and for ages, all over Europe, learning was considered unworthy of the warrior caste and was contemptuously referred to as the province of clerks and clerics. Indeed, it was the illiteracy of the nobility that gave the church such an enormous ascendency over the feudal lords of the Middle Ages.

This illiteracy and the consequences growing out of it is strikingly illustrated by Bulwer Lytton in "The Last of the Barons" in describing the struggle of Adam Warner, whose experiments with steam and the invention of an engine, led to suspicions that perhaps the Devil had a hand in it—a deduction that seemed almost confirmed when the engine blew up because it lacked a safety valve.

Tytler (History of Scotland) is authority for the statement that from the accession of Alexander III to the death of David (1370) it would be impossible to instance a single case of a Scottish baron possessing the power to sign his name. There is authority for the belief that this condition obtained in many cases, even as late as the closing half of the sixteenth century.

Arthur Young, whose valuable observations on France and French life and institutions have been made use of in the chapter dealing with the French Revolution, found such an amazing degree of ignorance in eighteenth century France that he easily persuaded a Frenchman that England possessed neither trees nor rivers.

Trade, industry, the useful arts, and the well-ordered life were despised in "the good old days," and war, outrage, pillage, and gross intemperance in eating and drinking were regarded as the only fit occupations of a gentleman. Indeed, although manners have softened, labour and trade are still held in contempt, and when a member of the nobility actually does go to work, it causes a ripple of excitement and long cabled accounts of the phenomenon to the foreign press give the incident international note.

As late as the eighteenth century (see

Hazlitt's "Old Cookery Books") the custom of using the fork at table—started in Italy in the fourteenth century—was still a novelty in England, and gentlemen travelling in Great Britain (see International Encyclopedia) who had acquired the habit on the Continent always carried a fork in a case, for the inns did not supply them. Hazlitt also inclines to give credence to the report that when Queen Elizabeth was told of the defeat of the Armada she was keeping "secret house" and enjoying an unconventional session with a roast goose. Keeping "secret house" was the way they characterized in those days a return to the rude manners of the "good old times" before table etiquette began to make inroads in England. If Mrs. Trollope had been more mindful of her own people's recent emergence from barbarism, she might have been kinder to the Yankees of the early nineteenth century whose habits she criticised so frankly in "Domestic Manners of the Americans."

It is not so many generations ago that ancestors of some of our "best" American families used to rush in at the dinner hour with coat off and suspenders down and tackle their tripe and corn cakes with all the wild abandon of primitive man.

Mediæval Lords of Have-and-Hold sometimes combined patronage of the Arts with the greatest cruelties of unrestrained despotism. Selwyn Brinton, author of "Renaissance in Italian Art," declares that when the Communes and Republics of Italy began to get exhausted and finally to disappear, there sprang up in their place everywhere, the great princely houses, the Medici of Florence, the Visconti and the Sforza at Milan, the Este at Ferrara, the Bentivogli at Bologna, the Montefeltri at Urbino, the Baglioni at Perugia, the Malatesta at Rimini, and Cesena and the Gonzaghi at Mantua—all living in castles, lording it over the adjacent territory, and forever in the shadow of death from poison or murder.

"In the strange and frightful isolation in which the Italian despot often lived," says Brinton, "ever plotting himself to keep his insecure throne, ever watching against plots within the city and without, this brilliant society of dependents (scholars, poets, painters) became his solace and his highest pleasure. Traverse that wonderful palace of the house of Este—intact, surrounded by its moat, dominating with its insolent pride the old city of Ferrara. Into the upper galleries and banquet halls the sunlight pours. We seem to hear the musical laughter, the rustle of the rich old cinque-cento costumes; the walls are hung with paintings by Dosso Dossi or Titian—naked wrestlers, figures running, and the radiant deities of the old re-awakened mythology.

"And below, beneath even the moat, lies the other side of the picture: the horrible dungeons, dark, noisome, shadowy, where the political conspirator, the inconvenient relative, the too outspoken citizen, the suspected wife, were thrust, and —soon forgotten."

In the "Life and Letters of Elizabeth, Last Duchess of Gordon," by the Rev. A. Moody Stuart, will be found the following incident abridged from Sir Walter Scott: "Two hundred years ago, Gordon Castle, then called the Bog of Gicht, presented a very different scene. The Farquharsons of Deeside having slain a Gordon of note, the Marquis of Huntly, along with the Laird of Grant, prepared to take a bloody vengeance for his death. That none of the guilty tribe might escape, Grant occupied the upper end of the vale of Dee with his clan while the Gordons ascended the river from beneath, each party killing, burning, and destroying without mercy all they found before them. The men and women of the race were nearly all slain; and when the day was done, Huntly found himself encumbered with about two hundred orphan children.

"About a year after the foray, the Laird of Grant chanced to dine at the Marquis's castle, and was of course entertained with magnificence. After dinner Huntly conducted Grant to a balcony which overlooked the kitchen, where he saw the remains of the abundant feast of the numerous household flung at random into a large trough. The master cook gave a signal with his silver whistle, on which a hatch like that of a dog kennel was raised, and there rushed into the kitchen, shrieking, shouting, yelling, a huge mob of children, half-naked and totally wild, who threw themselves on the contents of the trough, and fought, struggled, and clamored for the largest share.

"Grant was a man of humanity, and asked, 'In the name of Heaven, who are these?' 'They are the children of those Farquharsons whom we slew last year on Deeside,' answered Huntly.

"The Laird felt more shocked than it would have been prudent or polite to express. 'My Lord,' he said, 'my sword helped to make these poor children orphans, and it is not fair that your lordship should be burdened with all the expense of maintaining them. You have supported them for a year and a day, allow me now to take them to Castle Grant, and keep them for the same time at my cost.'

"Such was the savage sport of the lord of Gordon Castle two hundred years ago; and when his lady looked over that balcony, it was only to enjoy the spectacle, and not to rescue any of the wretched children from their revolting degradation."

Like father, like son; children of Lords of Have-and-Hold were equally unmindful of the feelings of the common people. In Eugene Sue's "The Iron Trevet," one of "The Mysteries of the People" series, he tells of a seignior's son who lamented that he had never seen a serf drowned. In the Clancarty there is handed down a tradition that a daughter of a Mac-Carthy More wept because she had never seen a peasant hanged. To please her, her father ordered a man brought in from the fields and his daughter's wish was soon satisfied.

The people as the demagogues love to call the mass of the Hathnaughts are easily gulled even in our day, and they permitted this injustice to go on in exchange for sops occasionally thrown to them.

Etienne De La Boetie (1530-1563) in a work called "Discourse on Voluntary Slavery," but also known as "Contre-Un" (Against One), which Warner's Library of the World's Best Literature describes as a rather flat attack on monarchy, but which nevertheless is filled with sound and shrewd observation, pays his respects to "the people." In common with many historians, De La Boetie notes how easily the people are made to forget their liberties and the outrages against them when they are lured by theatrical performances, games, spectacles, gladiatorial combats, and the exhibiting of strange beasts, as was the usual method among Roman tyrants to make the populace willing instruments of oppression. The tyrants used even to feast the Roman mob, and this appeal to appetite was so effective, says Boetie, that the "cleverest of them all would not have dropped his bowl of soup to recover the liberty of the Republic of Plato."

That feudal system of government in New York city known as Tammany Hall is founded on the same principle. Every year the district leaders give outings, and the allegiance of the enfranchised fools of the city is purchased for a plate of chowder.

Heinrich Heine (1799-1856), a very good friend of human liberty, likewise had contempt for the loafer proletariat. "Your poor Monarch" (the people), he says, "is not lovely; on the contrary, he is very ugly. But his ugliness is the result of dirt, and will vanish as soon as we erect public bathhouses where his Majesty, the People, can bathe gratis. A bit of soap will not prove amiss, and we shall then behold a smart looking People, a People indeed of the first water. . . . As soon as his High Mightiness has been properly fed, and has sated his appetite, he will smile on us with gracious condescension, just as the other monarchs do. . . . He bestows his affection and his confidence on those who shout the jargon of his own passions; while he reserves his hatred for the brave man who endeavours to reason and exalt him. . . . Give the People the choice between the most righteous of the righteous and the most wretched highway robber, and rest assured its cry will be, 'Give us Barabbas. Long live Barabbas!'

"The secret of this perversion is ignorance. This national evil we must endeavour to allay by means of public schools, where education, together with bread and butter and such other food as may be required, will be supplied free of expense."

Therein lies the whole secret of true progress — Education.   Man's greatest crime, often committed in the name of the Most High, has been the degradation of God's image.   Slavery, serfdom, the Indian Caste system, all handmaids of Ignorance, have been designed to hold man down to the brute level, but Education, the training and disciplining of his thinking powers, will put him in touch with the Infinite.

Knowledge of hygiene and sanitation will yet banish the slums and the White Plague, and Domestic Science with its fireless cookers, vacuum cleaners, dish and clothes washing machines is already emancipating woman from drudgery.

A growing impatience with the jack-assery of armaments is bringing about a marked decline in the war spirit, and the softening of human passions has banished torture from judicial inquiries and is bringing about prison reform and a loud call for the abolition of capital punishment which is always swift for the poor and slow to reach the powerful. Race and religious prejudices are dying out, and snobbery is coming to be regarded as a fair target for ridicule.   There is graft in high places, but all this will be corrected by the independent voter when the fetish of partisan government and allegiance is destroyed.

We are doing away with poorhouses and robbing old age of its terrors through pensions and insurance, and the day is not far distant when representative government will be genuinely what it implies.

Coeval, too, with the emancipation of man and woman, is coming the emancipation of the child and a growing sense that it possesses certain little rights that no one has any right to dispute and which many States now recognize. Through playgrounds, Boy Scouts, Campfire Girls, and other organizations, childhood is not only being made tolerable, but zestful and joyous.

We are getting down to fundamentals—the root of things. We are no longer content to make misery comfortable. Hitherto by means of charity, we have been putting vaseline on a cancer. Now we would uproot the cancer—do away with poverty and degradation altogether, and in the place of a purposeless proletariat, substitute a clean, healthy, self-reliant, and ambitious working class. Out of the ages of Servitude is coming the Age of Service. Unmindful of agitator or demagogue, the better elements of Capital and Labour are coming together as brothers and will yet solve the problem of work and wages.

Through struggle we have gained security of life against Whim. It now remains for us to establish the principle of Responsibility—the right of man to certainty of employment and full and equitable recompense for it, without injustice to any man or confiscation of his property.

Up to the present time the great governing force of the world has been Whim

—"God and my right," said the strong man with his heel on the neck of the lowly. Man is now becoming insistent that Whim shall be replaced by Responsibility —that the rights of the race as a whole shall count for more than the desires of any individual, even to the extent of pulling down his fences and levelling his ancestral castles if the public weal demands it, just as in a former age the law upheld the Whim of a Duchess of Sutherland who sought to improve the landscape by evicting hundreds of poor Scottish crofters and driving them into starvation and death.

Progress, that strange, inexplicable and irresistible force, working relentlessly, incessantly, through a Law of Inevitability, is whirling Man onward to his Destiny. Even the Music of the Spheres seems to take on something of the chant of the Marseillaise. After centuries of thraldom to superstition and ignorance, man is beginning to understand real freedom.

THE END.

WITNESSES SUMMONED TO TESTIFY

Obedient to the promptings of inherited beliefs and prejudices, often hideous and cruel, we are dead men's slaves. Tradition keeps us in grooves cut long ago for our ancestors. In studying the history of the common people, one cannot avoid the conclusion that had there never been widespread ignorance and superstition, there never would have been any tyranny or political injustice; and that the emancipation of man and the happiness of the race can only be achieved through education and the supremacy of the educated.

I once overheard a pompous and ignorant city official, looking over a popular, illustrated account of paleontology in a Sunday newspaper, ask a better mentally equipped associate to define the difference between the dinosaurus and the ichthyosaurus. The man interrogated told him that the difference was almost imperceptible—the only distinction being that the dinosaurus had a binomial equation on its logarithm.

As this was said in all earnestness, the explanation was accepted. That city official was a true descendant of the fellow who proposed to breed gondolas. What can be expected in the way of good government from gentlemen like that? While we have ignorant statesmen and an ignorant citizenship, all the socialism that has ever been preached will not remedy conditions.

Until mankind learns to appreciate the useful, and recognizes the ennobling effect of work, we will have the spectacle of the gilded youth wasting his substance on chorus girls, and sturdy loafers supported by the washtub energy of wives, mothers, and sisters. Against such, rich and poor, the vagrancy laws should be enforced.

In this account of the struggle between Dennis Hathnaught and the Lords of Have-and-Hold, it has been necessary to summon many witnesses. Among those that have testified may be cited the following:

Lubbock's "Prehistoric Times" and "Origin of Civilization"; Drummond's "Ascent of Man"; Morgan's "Ancient Society"; Reade's "Martyrdom of Man"; Sir Henry Sumner Maine's Works; Tylor's "Early History of Mankind" and "Primitive Culture"; Charles Darwin's Works; Flquier's "Primitive Man"; Aeschylus' "Prometheus Bound"; Hesiod's "Works and Days"; Herodotus' History; The Bible; Livy's "History of Rome"; Plutarch's Lives; Theognis; Aristotle's "Politics"; Aristophanes' Comedies; Plato's "Republic"; Xenophon's "Economics"; International Encyclopedia; Flaubert's "Salammbo"; Fowler's "Social Life at Rome in the Age of Cicero"; Motley's "Rise of the Dutch Republic"; Webster's Dictionary.

Buckle's "History of Civilization"; Charles Rann Kennedy's "Servant in the House"; Thucydides' "History of the Peloponnesian War"; Keightley's "History of Greece"; Thirlwall's "History of Greece"; Encyclopædia Britannica; Mommsen's "History of Rome"; Juvenal's Satires; Gibbon's "Decline and Fall of the Roman Empire"; Ferraro's "Greatness and Decline of Rome"; Ward's "Pure Sociology"; Edward Everett's Works; Duruy's "Middle Ages"; Robertson's "History of Charles, the Fifth"; Hallam's Middle Ages"; Hecker's "Epidemics of the Middle Ages"; Eugene Sue's "Mysteries of the People" series (De Leon translation)"; Bonnemere's "Histoire des Paysans"; Freeman's "History of the Norman Conquest of England"; Green's "History of the English People''; Scott's ''Ivanhoe''; Taine's ''History of English Literature''; Sanderson's ''History of the World''; Hackwood's ''The Good Old Times''; Hume's ''History of England''; Knowles' ''William Tell''; Guizot's ''History of Civilization in Europe''; Menzel's ''History of Germany''; Chaucer; Wicklif's Bible; Froude's ''History of England''; Harrison's ''Description of England''; Abbott's ''Common People of Ancient Rome''; Smith's ''English Guilds''; Macaulay's ''History of England''; General Stewart's ''Sketches of the Highlanders.''

Rousseau's ''Political Economy''; Fielding's ''Tom Jones''; Linton's ''George Eliot'' in ''Women Novelists of the Reign of Victoria''; Toynbee's ''Industrial Revolution''; Reade's ''Put Yourself in His Place''; Lockhart's ''Life of Napoleon Buonaparte''; Gibbins' ''Industrial History of England''; French Revolution—Taine, De-Tocqueville, Thiers, Blanc, Van Laun, Lamartine, Rocquain, Arthur Young, Mignet, Doniol, Michelet, Alison, Sybel, Hausser, Rabaut, Buchez, Kerverseau and Clavelin, Ternaux, Madame de Stael, Janet, Burke, Quinet, Berriat, Mackintosh, Croker, Dickens, Rousseau, Voltaire, Carlyle; Isham's ''The Mud Cabin''; London Chronicle; Alison's ''History of Europe''; Dean Swift; Lytton's ''My Novel''; McCarthy's ''History of Our Own Times''; Westminster Gazette; G. K. Chesterton; Manchester Guardian; A. St. John Adcock; English Government Reports and Blue Books; Sir Francis Galton, the eugenist; McCarthy's Anti-Clerical Works on Ireland; Lover's ''Rory O'More''; Lecky's ''Leaders of Public Opinion in Ireland''; Wendell Phillips' oration on O'Connell; Winston Churchill's Home Rule Speech at Belfast; Rambaud's ''History of Russia''; Gogol's ''Dead Souls''; Turgenief's ''Mumu''; Voltaire's ''Charles XII.''

New York Sun; Campbell's ''Pleasures of Hope''; Cobden's ''Political Writings''; Hildreth's ''History of the United States''; Hawthorne's ''Scarlet Letter''; McMaster's ''History of the People of the United States''; Tarbell's ''History of the Standard Oil Company''; Jeremy Bentham; George Frisbie Hoar; Cairnes' ''The Slave Power''; Wallon's ''History of Slavery''; Sienkiewicz's ''Quo Vadis''; De Tocqueville's ''Democracy in America''; Mark Twain's ''Life on the Mississippi''; The British Constitution; Brinton's ''Renaissance in Italian Art''; Stuart's ''Life of the Duchess of Gordon''; Boetie's ''Voluntary Slavery'' (Against One); Heinrich Heine; Rogers' ''Six Centuries of Work and Wages''; Webb's ''History of Trade Unionism''; Brentano's ''Guilds and Trade Unions''; Fawcett's ''Political Economy''; David Livingstone; Lasalle; Herberman's ''Business Life in Ancient Rome''; Rousseau's ''Social Contract''; Esquiros' ''Evangel of the People''; Karl Marx's ''Capital''; Hawthorne's ''Blithedale Romance''; Spielhagen's ''Hammer and Anvil''; Bebel's ''Woman and Labour''; Moffat's ''Bunty Pulls the Strings''; The Knights of

Columbus; Industrial Workers of the World; New York Evening Post; H. C. Lea's "History of the Inquisition"; Wiseman's "Fabiola."

Clay's "Syndicalism and Labour"; Lewis' "Syndicalism and the General Strike"; Brooks' "American Syndicalism"; Tridon's "New Unionism"; Swedenborg; Browning; Walt Whitman; George's "Progress and Poverty"; Harper's Magazine; Quesnay and the Physiocrats; Adam Smith; Herbert Spencer; Malthus on "Population"; Morley's "Diderot and the Encyclopedists"; Woods' "Metzerott, Shoemaker"; Barr's "The Mutable Many"; Ditchfield's "Old English Squire"; Hay's "The Breadwinners"; Norris' "The Octopus" and "The Pit"; Churchill's "The Inside of the Cup"; Lytton's "Last of the Barons"; Tytler's "History of Scotland"; Hazlitt's "Old Cookery Books"; Mrs. Trollope's "Domestic Manners of the Americans"; Davitt's "Within the Pale"; Grote's "History of Greece"; Ferguson's "Greek Imperialism."